Escape to Freedom

Leon Rubinstein

Foreword by Michael Berenbaum

Hamilton Books
A member of
The Rowman & Littlefield Publishing Group
Lanham • Boulder • New York • Toronto • Plymouth, UK

Copyright © 2007 by
Hamilton Books
4501 Forbes Boulevard
Suite 200
Lanham, Maryland 20706
Hamilton Books Acquisitions Department (301) 459-3366

Estover Road
Plymouth PL6 7PY
United Kingdom

Library of Congress Control Number: 2007922018
ISBN-13: 978-0-7618-3691-9 (paperback : alk. paper)
ISBN-10: 0-7618-3691-8 (paperback : alk. paper)

∞™ The paper used in this publication meets the minimum
requirements of American National Standard for Information
Sciences—Permanence of Paper for Printed Library Materials,
ANSI Z39.48—1984

Tomorrow, when stillness will descend
Upon these killing fields
And cries of our slaughtered people
Are no longer heard
Know that their fear was not of death alone
But that the world would not remember
That they lived

Contents

Contents

Foreword

Memoirs by Holocaust survivors have proliferated in recent years, quality works by men and women determined to fulfill their obligation to those they left behind and to bequeath their memories to the future. It is a race against death and also a means of approaching death, drawing closer to that mysterious end.

Survivors are no strangers to death. It surrounded them during the years of darkness when they saw it firsthand. By luck and circumstances, yet surely not without skill and determination, they avoided it and lived. Many survivors are surprised to be regarded as heroes, admired for their resilience and determination by young people in the early twenty-first century. They intuitively understand that by committing their memories to paper, they can gain a measure of mastery over their past and achieve some sense, however inadequate, of closure.

Once their condition was perilous because a persistent and powerful enemy was bent on their destruction and they found the inner resources to endure. Afterwards—and for some, a very long time afterwards—they found the strength to begin again.

Once they were victims. Make no mistake about it: even those who survived were victims. Perhaps, especially those who survived were victims, for theirs was the difficult task of bridging between that world and our world, of living with haunting memories, unheroic memories.

Upon arrival in the lands of their freedom, they became refugees. In Palestine and after 1948, Israel, they went from camps to the battlefield, from one form of attack to another. In the United States, they were told to take their place as the latest in a long line of refugees who faced oppression elsewhere and came to these shores to rebuild their lives in freedom.

The uniqueness of their experience, however, was not appreciated for many years.

Over time, they became known as survivors, modern "Isaacs" who faced the slaughter and saw the dark side of God and humanity. Like the least known of our biblical patriarchs, survivors who had a knife to their throat were granted a reprieve. There was a special quality to their existence, special meaning. Being intimate with death, some deeply knew how to embrace life while others struggled to live their lives despite death.

Now in old age, with children grown, careers completed, grandchildren beckoning them to tell of the past and to speak to the future, many have transformed survival into witness, offering their stories as testimony, as a lesson and a warning.

Because they have faced death, many will have learned what is most important in life—life itself, love, family and community. The small things, the simple things we all take for granted, are not taken for granted. They are treasured and appreciated anew.

Leon Rubinstein has offered us a simple, yet powerful memoir. He has told his story. The only son of a poor family, he recalls the burdens of that poverty. He writes of his father with clarity and understanding, with sympathy and love, but not with aggrandizement or false heroism. He writes of himself as a child in Nazi Germany who experienced the rise of Hitler through taunts in the schools and dangers that loomed as he walked the streets. He depicts the attack on his father's meager store—the broken glass that told them it was time to leave. Ironically, because they had so little, they could leave; they could have as little elsewhere where the dangers were less. He writes of their escape from Germany. His parents had the wisdom to leave early, but the misfortune to have real safety elude them time and again. The prominent journalist Dorothy Thompson once wrote of her era: "It is a sad commentary on the nature of a time that a stamp in a passport is the difference between life and death." The visa for America that the Rubinstein family sought was always soon to be forthcoming, but never soon enough.

He writes of life in Belgium with his parents, and then of life in France. As German Jewish refugees with few resources, they muddled through. It was a meager existence, not without its pain and not without its indignities, but it seemed tolerable compared to what had been left behind. Many people helped. For any Jew to survive, help was essential and when it was forthcoming it was often offered graciously and selflessly. He writes of the loss of his father, who was deported to a transit camp and then on to Auschwitz where he was murdered, one of the six million. Leon, then a teen-aged boy, was left with his mother; she was to care for him, and in the topsy-turvy world of the Holocaust, he was left to care for her.

The Talmud invokes a principle of Scriptural interpretation: "Were it not explicitly written, we could never have said it." Permit me to suggest a principle of understanding the Shoah: "If it did not actually happen, one would never have dared write it even in fiction." Much of what happened would have been literally incredible—something that could not be believed. Leon's story is both incredible—and truthful.

The story of Leon's escape with his mother to Switzerland would have challenged even an experienced novelist: travel with false papers on trains and buses; their desperation to reach a border village; entering the thicket of danger by traveling with two German soldiers from one town to another when even the slightest of missteps, even one word from his mother's accented tongue, would have meant incarceration and deportation to death; the lonely trek up the snow-capped mountain, where on one side there was death and on the other side, freedom—if only one could elude the patrols, if only one was not betrayed by the smugglers who guided people across the border. He was young, a teen-aged boy at the height of his physical prowess. His mother was a fragile middle-aged woman pained by arthritis and limited by a weak heart, yet mother and son walked on together as one. Along the way, we meet silent heroes, men and women who offered food or shelter, information or even money that enabled the mother and son to go on.

Writing with restraint and with care, Leon does not embellish the story. Still one can feel the danger and then the sense the exaltation of crossing that border, of reaching freedom and with freedom, opportunity—the opportunity to recover physically, to resume his education interrupted long ago, to dream of a different world and less ominous time, and to love.

Now a man of more than four score years, Leon Rubinstein writes of the love of his youth with the passion of youth and the innocence of youth. Ultimately he must choose between his mother and his lover, between the United States and Palestine. The differences were stark, the choices anguished.

When I first read this book, Leon ended his memoir in the 1940s, depriving his reader of the understanding of what happened next. He had written of *before*. He had written of *during*. He had said almost nothing of *after*. The reader was left to imagine the rest. So in response to my pleas, Leon sketched in the raw outlines of the last three score years of his life in the United States. He still leaves much to the imagination, much unsaid and untold, but he offers us enough to understand that after building a life in the United States, undertaking a successful career and reaching the age of retirement, he chose to bear witness—to tell his story, to teach young people, in the hope that they can build a different future in a troubled world. He is the paradigmatic example of the survivor as witness and teacher.

For the experience of near death to have ultimate meaning, it must take shape in how one rebuilds from the ashes. Leon offers us one way, his example.

Michael Berenbaum

Los Angeles, California
April 2006

Preface

September 2, 1942, 8:35 a.m.: A train is leaving the Bourget-Drancy station near Paris.

One thousand and sixteen men, women and children are on that train. This is no ordinary train. The original reddish color is barely visible under a coat of heavy black soot. Steel bars are across each door with just a small barbed wire slat letting in a faint light. The destination is not known to the passengers, only the direction: EAST.

The train will cross the Franco-German border near Neuberg close to midnight. On September 4, at 5:33 a.m., the train will arrive at a place called Auschwitz. From the arriving passengers, 113 women will be selected for work and the numbers 19003 to 19115 will be tattooed on their forearms. Only 10 men, numbers 63055 to 63064, will be chosen for work. All other deportees, including all children, will immediately be sent to the gas chambers.

Among them was my father, Nathan Rubinstein. He was forty-eight years old.

It has been sixty-three years. The rage that once consumed me, has given way to a lingering sadness. Over the years I have accompanied him in my mind and I have shared the humiliation of being herded into a space that forced him to stand, all day and all night, throughout that fateful journey. I have smelled the fetid stench of filth and fear. My throat was parched; my lips were swollen for lack of water. My face was bathed in tears that would not stop. And I was with him when they pushed him into the gas chamber.

I am dedicating this book to the memory of my father and to the millions who were murdered in the Holocaust, the event columnist George Will called "the ultimate obscenity to mankind."

My father was a kind and orderly man in a world where kindness and order had disappeared. Over the past fifteen years I have told his story and the
history of those dark times, both in print and in the classroom, to thousands
of students throughout the Florida school system. I have been deeply touched
by their sensitivity and empathy and their desire to learn more about the
Holocaust.

Sometimes, a student would ask why, after so many years, I still have not
found closure to that tragic chapter. It is a legitimate question. For a long time
I had kept those memories bottled up, trying to leave that part of my past behind me as I embarked on a new life in my adopted country.

Then, on a trip to New York, I decided to visit the United Nations building.
One of the guides pointed out a small, secluded park across the street, which
he called an "oasis." The park was named after a Swedish diplomat who, in
the last days of the war, had saved thousands of Hungarian Jews by giving
them Swedish identity cards, thus placing them under the protection of a neutral country just as they were to be rounded up for deportation. His name was
Raoul Wallenberg.

On the south wall of that tree-lined square, I found a bronze plaque. It's in-
scription read:

Remember
Men, women, children, masses for the gas chambers
advancing toward horror beneath the whip of the executioner
Your sad Holocaust is engraved in history
and nothing shall purge your deaths from our memories
For our memories are your only grave

Indeed, our memories are their only grave! Who will remember when the
survivors are no longer here to testify? I therefore shall continue, as long as
God grants me the strength, to teach the history of those sad days when prejudice and discrimination, the twin cancers of the soul, fanned by unbridled
hatred, led to that black hole into which part of humanity vanished forever.

It is my fervent hope that a seed will have been planted in the minds and
hearts of the young. Their perception of who we are and how we are all in-
terdependent will be a catalyst in making this a better world.

Acknowledgments

This book, written in the evening of my life, is above all a remembrance of a time when an entire continent was shrouded in utter evil. Of families torn apart forever. Of youth lost. Of dreams never fulfilled.

And of that remarkable resilience man is capable of in order to survive.

I am grateful to my friend, Michael Berenbaum, a scholar who has devoted his life to making sure that the darkest chapter in human history is not forgotten. His guidance and advice were invaluable to a first-time author. I thank him for his unfaltering belief in my ability to tackle and complete this project, and for the generous giving of his time.

My thanks also go to my many friends who helped me to stay the course whenever I felt overwhelmed by the scope of the undertaking.

Above all, I thank my wife Renee, who has shared my life for fifty-five years, and our small family, without whose support and encouragement this book so dear to my heart could not have been written.

In order to present a faithful accounting of the historic events mentioned, I availed myself of some of the best documentation on the subject. They include:

Josephine Bacon: *The Illustrated Atlas of Jewish Civilization* (New York: Macmillan, 1990)

Michael Berenbaum: *The World Must Know: The History of the Holocaust as Told in the United States Holocaust Memorial Museum* (Boston: Little, Brown, 1993)

Martin Gilbert: *Israel: A History* (New York: Morrow, 1998)

Nora Levin: *The Holocaust: The Destruction of European Jewry 1933-1945* (New York: T. Y. Crowell, 1968)

Daniel J. Schroeter: *Israel: An Illustrated History* (New York: Oxford University Press, 1998)

The Holocaust Chronicle: A History in Words and Pictures (Lincolnwood, IL: Publications International Ltd., 2000)

Chapter One

Leaving Frankfurt

It was on a Sunday, early in May of 1933—I remember that day as if it happened yesterday—when a stone was thrown into my father's household store, smashing the window, causing the glass to shatter into a thousand pieces and land within inches of where I was standing. I recall my father's face turning white. He had been sitting behind a desk, absorbed in sorting out bills. My heart was racing and I could not stop trembling. I was ten years old.

My father walked over to me and took me into his arms. "Are you all right?" he asked. I nodded Then he went to a closet, took out a broom and started to sweep up the glass. I looked at him in bewilderment.

After a while, we ventured outside. The street was deserted. On the unbroken part of the glass pane, the outline of a Star of David that the vandals had spray-painted was still noticeable. My father went back into the store and removed a folder from a desk drawer. He motioned me to follow him as he walked out, having made sure to lock up. He did nothing to secure that gaping hole.

On the way home, I was holding on to his hand, not letting go until we reached our place.

Frankfurt am Main was home to the second largest Jewish community in Germany since the early part of the twentieth century. We lived here, in a small apartment on a quiet street.

From our second floor window, I had a panoramic view of a park in which the Goethe House was located, the birthplace of Germany's greatest poet. Across from the park, a number of stores were scattered among apartment buildings. My favorite one was the candy store, a place I would pass on my way to school. Sometimes the owner stood in front of it, and waving me to step inside, grabbed a candy bar from a jar and handed it to me. "Now work

1

hard today," he would admonish me with a big smile. Every ten minutes a streetcar came churning along, carefully turning the corner, while emitting the muffled sound of a warning bell.

Like the rest of the world, Germany was in the throes of a severe economic depression. The unemployment rate reached 25 percent of the work force and the heavy reparations imposed by the allies after World War I made the country a fertile ground for the rise of a fanatic rabble-rouser.

From 1930, when Hitler's National Socialist Party managed to win 107 seats in the Reichstag (the German parliament), to January 1933, when it emerged as Germany's leading party and Hitler became Chancellor, life for Jews in Germany changed dramatically. Up to that time, Jews had shared in the hardships of the rest of the population. Most of them belonged to the Social Democratic Party and while a latent antisemitism had never disappeared, many of them, especially those who had fought in the World War I, often declared themselves to be Germans first and Jews second.

As an only child with few friends, I spent hours daydreaming, looking out the window, imagining cowboys in white hats charging down the street in pursuit of Indians armed with bows and arrows. When Hitler came to power, appointed by the old Marshall Von Hindenburg of World War I fame, my fantasy was replaced with a new reality.

Suddenly the streets below were teeming with thousands of men in brown shirts, carrying large banners with swastikas, marching in their black boots while singing the Horst Wessel song, dedicated to the memory of a thug who was killed in a gun fight. Night and day the airwaves resonated with diatribes against the Jews, blaming them for all of Germany's troubles: "Die Juden sind unser Unglueck," the Jews are our misfortune.

I found myself glued to the radio and one day I asked my father, "Papa, are we bad people?"

"Why do you ask such a question?" he wanted to know.

"All these stories on the radio and those terrible drawings in the newspapers of ugly, old men, sucking the blood out of Christian babies to make matzos. I know it is not true, but why are they saying it?"

"No," he replied, his eyes filled with sadness. "We are not bad people, they are!"

My father owned a small household store on a narrow street in the old part of the city. When my mother's father died, he left her some money, just enough for a down payment on the place. They called it the "95 Pfennig Bazaar." With just one narrow show window, the store was so small that most people would just walk past it. Pots and pans hung from hooks along the entrance, while the window displayed several sets of dishes on a table with price tags that my father had drawn with great precision.

On Sundays, he often took me to the store and gave me a few chores, like sweeping out and arranging merchandise. I was proud that he trusted me to help him.

Because of the many Woolworth stores and the German version, the EHP, my father's store could not compete with the enormous variety and the low prices they had to offer. Business became worse every month and the handwriting was on the wall. Many a night, as I lay awake in a small room next to their bedroom, I heard my parents talking about their worries and fears—how the suppliers were pressing them to pay the bills and how the landlord threatened them with eviction if the rent was not paid within ten days. I learned that my parents had borrowed money from friends and family members and that even they had reminded them to start making payments.

One morning, just before Christmas, a man in a black overcoat carrying a bulky briefcase came to the apartment and proceeded to affix a decal with an official stamp on the back of our beautiful teakwood credenza with mahogany inlay, a wedding gift from my mother's parents. He was claiming it for unpaid debts. A few days later, two burly men lugged the ten-foot long piece down the stairs and loaded it on a large truck. I can still see my mother looking down from the window behind the drapes, sobbing quietly and my father putting his arms around her, trying to console her.

Soon after, we moved into a one-room apartment, where we had some kitchen privileges. The bath was at the end of the hallway.

I was a third grade student at the Philantropin, a Jewish school, located just ten minutes from where we lived. After school, I sometimes encountered a group of the Hitler Youth in their brown shirts and their armbands with the swastika on it. They had a special routine, waiting on street corners for Jewish kids on their way home. "Look at that Jew," their leader, a rather tall eleven-year-old would exclaim. "He walks on our German sidewalk!" When I stepped into the street, he said, "Now he is on our German street!" It usually ended with the bunch pushing and shoving me, until I fell to the ground. When I was walking with another schoolmate, who happened to take the same route, the group refrained from attacking us. They did not like the odds of four against two.

I tried to take a different way home, but they often managed to catch up with me. I never told my parents about my ordeal. I felt that I had to handle it myself. One day, when I was again confronted by my persecutors and the leader was about to start his taunting, I raised my fist and landed it squarely on his mouth. I can still see his surprised look as he wiped away the blood from his lips.

After that I do not recall too much. When I did not show up at home on time, my mother went looking for me and found me slumped on the grass. I needed some stitches and stayed home for a few days.

There had also been numerous incidents of old, bearded Jewish men being forced to scrub the sidewalk after the Nazis had poured white paint on it. Many were beaten when they failed to clean up the spill fast enough.

My encounter with the Hitler Youth convinced my parents to seriously start planning to leave Germany. "I will try to have someone take that store off my hands," my father said.

That was before that fateful Sunday morning when our store was attacked. When we walked through the door, my mother looked up in surprise. We never had been back that early before. She immediately knew that something was wrong by the way we dragged ourselves in before plunking down on the couch. Haltingly, my father gave her an account of what had happened and how close I had come to being injured. Without uttering a word, she pulled two suitcases from a closet and started to fill them up with clothes. We both looked on in silence. Finally my father said, "Yes, it is time to leave!"

We packed our few belongings and said good-bye to our friends and relatives. Two weeks later, we took the train to the border town of Kehl. Carrying our suitcases, we walked across the bridge over the Rhine separating Kehl from the French town of Strasburg, capital of the province of Alsace. In those days, it was still possible to get an exit permit and an entrance visa, although the French authorities stipulated that we had to move away from the border areas within three months.

Chapter Two

Luxembourg and Brussels

The Grand Duchy of Luxembourg is a tiny country, the shape of a shoe, surrounded by Belgium, Germany and France. Half the size of Delaware, it has one of the highest standards of living today, and even back in the thirties, most of its "burghers" lived a rather comfortable life.

The country has an interesting history. Once more than triple its present size, called the County of Luxembourg, it gradually got smaller and smaller as its neighbors bit off pieces. In the process, the surrounding countries promoted it to first a "Duchy," and then a "Grand Duchy." It is said that the inhabitants were deadly afraid of becoming citizens of a "Kingdom"—with just about the capital left.

When we moved there from Strasbourg in the summer of 1933, we did so in the hope of making it our temporary stop on the way to the United States, where my father's brother was a watchmaker in the Bronx. He promised to send us the affidavits and guarantees needed to obtain the coveted visa.

Most European countries had vastly divergent policies toward the Jewish refugees who had fled Germany—and later Austria—when Hitler came to power. While we were allowed to reside in Luxembourg, my father was not permitted to work there. He therefore found a job as a traveling salesman in Switzerland some 150 miles to the south, where he secured a work permit but no permanent residence. He would spend two to three months, traveling from town to town throughout Switzerland, trying to sell linens as part of a dowry to prospective brides, often from door to door.

My father was a shy and gentle man, not given to the glibness and smoothness that were needed to clinch the sale. There was little money coming our way and I learned early on what it meant to do without. I dreaded the first of each month, when the rent was due; the landlord became increasingly impatient and often verbally abusive when we were late.

5

My mother would visit some of our more comfortable friends and sometimes come back with a small amount. I do not know when and if these
amounts were paid back. Slowly, though, these resources would dry up. At
night I heard my mother sobbing, as she lay awake trying to find a way for us
to survive.

It hurt me very much to see her so despondent. There had always been a
sadness about her. I could not recall her ever bursting out laughing. Even
when her lips were smiling, her eyes were not.

Once in a while, a small gold coin came in the mail from America. It was
from my uncle Max, my father's brother. It was literally a godsend. Somehow
we managed to muddle through. My father would sometimes stay away for as
long as two months before he came to visit us for a few days. It all depended
on how much commission he had earned. Most of the time he just sent whatever he could, after paying for his expenses, and there was nothing left for the
train fare.

It was an absurd setup, to have two households when we could not even afford one, but those were the restrictions we were dealing with in the two
countries. We were still hopeful that Luxembourg would eventually give my
father a work permit and he would no longer have to travel to Switzerland.

Our time was measured by the letters we exchanged with my uncle. There
seemed to be an ever-increasing number of requirements asked of him; his in-
come was modest and no visa came our way.

In 1936, I became a bar mitzvah in the only synagogue in Luxembourg.
The rabbi, Dr. Serebrenik, originally from Vienna, conducted the service. As
I stood at the *bima*, reading my *parsha,* the Torah portion that I had memo-
rized, I saw high up in the balcony my beautiful mother, smiling at me. She
wore a pale blue silk dress that she had sewn herself from remnants she had
found on sale. My father stood to my left, his black hat shiny from wear. His
only dark suit, though carefully pressed, looked shabby. I felt terrible because
my parents had sold the silver candlesticks they had kept all these years in order to buy my navy blue suit for the occasion.

In his sermon, the rabbi told me: "Go to Palestine, work with your hands,
till the earth, help build a nation and become part of a wonderful future." It
would be nearly fifty years before I made that journey the rabbi had admonished me to undertake.

In a room adjacent to the sanctuary, a small party was given for me by my
uncle Sigmund, my mother's brother, who also had fled from Frankfurt to
Luxembourg. A handful of my friends from school attended. I received the
customary fountain pen and a silver cigarette case engraved with my initials
that I would never use.

In early July, the long awaited letter finally arrived. When my father saw the envelope from the American consulate, he tore it open with trembling hands. Glancing at the contents, his eyes lit up.

"We got it!" he exclaimed full of excitement, "It's the invitation to pick up the visa. Thank God, our prayers have been answered!" The appointment date was for July 12, just three days away.

On that morning we took the train from Brussels to Antwerp, the site of the consulate, a short one-hour ride, and we soon stood in front of the building situated in a cul-de-sac. The sight of the Stars and Stripes fluttering from a flagpole filled us with joy and a sense of accomplishment.

During the next few hours we were sent from one office to the next, filling out endless papers and winding up in a doctor's office where we had to undergo the required and rather lengthy medical examination.

It was noon when we were ushered into a large room with high ceilings and motioned to sit on one of the benches lined up in front of a dark wooden desk standing on a platform. We were the only people in the room. On the wall facing us hung a picture of President Franklin Roosevelt with his pince-nez and a cigarette holder dangling from his lips, looking at us with that famous smile. An American flag stood next to the desk. The opposite wall was almost completely covered with a gigantic map of the forty-eight states.

The door opened and a portly, balding man in his fifties entered and took a seat in a swivel chair. Shuffling some papers, he looked down on us with a big grin. "Well, Mr. Rubinstein," he said in a booming voice, "you finally made it! Your medical exam came out fine. Everything is in order and we are ready to welcome you to the United States of America."

At that moment the door opened again and a tall man in a brown suit entered the room. He had gray cropped hair and rimless glasses. Without as much as giving us a glance, he walked over to the consul and whispered something in his ear.

The consul seemed startled. Turning his back toward us, he engaged in an exchange of words, inaudible to us. The man in the brown suit kept on shaking his head and after a while, he simply walked out. For a few moments the consul sat motionless. When he finally looked at us, clearing his voice, we felt a sudden chill in the air. "I am sorry," he said, and we could tell he meant it, "but the quota for this year has been closed, you must come back next year."

My father jumped up. "What do you mean, sir?" he exclaimed. "You have just congratulated us on getting the visa!"

"I am sorry," he kept on saying, now avoiding looking at us, "but there is nothing that can be done. The quota is closed as of this moment."

My father walked the few steps leading to the desk and grabbing the consul's hand, he started to implore him. For the first time in my life I hated my father.

"Don't you see, it is useless," I said, getting up and pulling him away. "Let's go."

We walked through the streets of Antwerp, its trees in bloom that summer day, with tears in our eyes and pain in our hearts. "There will be another day," I tried to sound confident, but somehow I did not sound very convincing, even to myself.

What we did not know then, was that my father had just been sentenced to death.

Four years later, at a place called Auschwitz, the sentence would be carried out.

Whenever my father came to spend a few days with us, it was like a special holiday for me. After school, we would take long walks, just the two of us. There were visits to the zoo or a museum. We would explore the marvels of the world and talk about a multitude of subjects. Miraculously our daily hardships receded during those walks. There were so many things I wanted to know and my father responded to all my inquiries with a wealth of knowledge and a tongue-in-cheek humor. He was a lover of opera and early on introduced me to some of the great arias and their interpreters. He had a decent voice and would sing for me the most memorable passages.

For my thirteenth birthday, my parents had bought me a ticket to *Carmen*. Much as they would have liked to accompany me, they could only afford one ticket. Sitting all the way up in the balcony, I experienced my first opera; I remember I was thrilled by the entrance of the Toreador to Bizet's melodic music and fascinated by the tragic demise of Carmen at the hand of her lover, Don Jose.

My father was a whiz in geography and could draw the map of Europe from memory and nearly to scale. I soon managed to remember all capitals and duly impressed my classmates. He also introduced me to the beauty of literature. I became an avid reader, tackling such authors as Hemingway, Steinbeck, Upton Sinclair, Dostoevsky and Stendahl, some of it a bit above my head. I recall his telling me the story of Goethe's *Faust*. I was puzzled and repulsed by Faust selling his soul to the devil, just to regain his youth. Though I still dislike the idea, I now have some understanding of his motive.

But my father wasn't only interested in cerebral things. We were both avid soccer fans and faithfully attended the matches of our home team. My mother knew at once when we walked through the door whether our team had won or lost. We either marched in utter silence, or else we'd joke and tell of the exploits of our favorite players.

And of course, we spoke of the times we lived in. Though he usually tried to be upbeat, he now was deeply pessimistic about the future. How right he was, we soon would find out.

Marty Ohrbach was a friend of my father's who lived in Brussels where he had a linen business. He had visited us a few times in Luxembourg. A week after our meeting with the consul, Marty called and told us that a shirt manufacturer and former associate of his was looking for a traveling salesman.

"This is a great opportunity for you," Marty told my father. "You would get a salary against a commission with all expenses paid. You can bring your family to Brussels and will be able to work and reside in the same place."

We were truly elated. My mother wanted to know how this would work out with my schooling. Marty assured her that there would be no problem switching from the lycée in Luxembourg, as the curriculum, with the exception of the language courses, was nearly identical. While French was the main language in both countries, German was the second language in Luxembourg and Flemish in Belgium. Anxious to get a new start, we made the move in two weeks.

For the next few days we were busy looking for an apartment similar to the one we had left behind. We were fortunate to find a suitable place in a low priced residential area.

Brussels turned out to be a lovely, buzzing city, with wide boulevards, beautiful stores and sidewalk cafes at every corner where a colorful crowd watched the world go by while sipping their favorite apéritif.

My father had met his boss in Liège where the shirt factory was located and had come back, quite pleased with that encounter. Our friends, the Ohrbachs, were very helpful in getting us settled and for the first time since our emigration, things began to look up. Nevertheless, the prospect of going back to school, after having come that close to leaving Europe behind, was quite depressing to me.

I still had some six weeks left and decided to become a volunteer to help the Spanish Republicans who had been defeated by Franco in a civil war that brought thousands of refugees to France, Belgium and the few neighboring countries willing to give asylum to these early victims of fascism. I had followed the civil war with great interest, as it became clear that both Hitler and Mussolini were using that war as a testing ground.

After registering at the office that trained volunteers, I was given a sign and a metal coin box and soon was standing at the corner of Rue Neuve in the center of Brussels, approaching passers-by with a plea to support the victims of that war. My parents were not very enchanted, since they felt that I ran the risk of encountering the opposing factions, who were also quite visible in the city at that time.

One day, an elderly gentleman approached me and said: "You are working for a good cause." He introduced himself and told me that he was the rabbi of a small congregation. After I gave him my name, he suggested that I might want to work for the Jewish Committee for the refugees who had come from Austria and Germany during the last few years as more and more Jews were persecuted and Hitler's attacks in the press and on the radio increased at a frenetic pace.

The committee was located at Rue des Tanneurs, in the predominantly Jewish quarter of the city. Here I became a stock clerk, working some thirty hours a week, carrying files from one office to another. In the process, I made the acquaintance of hundreds of refugees and their families, who lined up daily to receive financial aid or who needed assistance in finding a country that would accept them as the authorities had only granted them a temporary visa.

Others had serious medical problems or needed help getting jobs, which was a difficult task because of the dire economic conditions and the already high unemployment rate in Belgium. I soon became familiar with the entire process and my bosses seemed to be pleased with my work.

I noticed that little was being done for the children between the ages of eight and sixteen when they were not in school. The parents had no money left for any leisure activities and the committee planned nothing for them. I went to the director and suggested giving these youngsters a place to get together in the building that housed the office. He was very receptive to my idea and found us a small room. I then approached a number of wealthy Belgian Jews, whose names had been given to me, and submitted to them my plan for providing some after-school activities for these youngsters on afternoons and on weekends. To make this a more self-sustaining venture, I asked for permission to publish a small newspaper using a hand press.

In this newspaper, I described current sport events and wrote about countries that might become a haven for some of the refugees trying to emigrate. The paper met with rather surprising success. Most of our customers, seeing the positive results, would make a generous contribution, far in excess of its selling price of five francs. Soon we were able to take some twenty youngsters to soccer matches, swimming pools and other events, including an occasional movie. In no time the club attracted an ever-increasing number of youngsters, happy to escape for a few hours the often dreary and confining environment where they lived with their parents and siblings. Part of the money also went for books and indoor sports equipment.

I shared the running of this "Cercle des Enfants Réfugiés," as I called it, with a few older boys and girls. We also started a small theatre group with the help of some very talented kids and performed at the small nearby theatre that graciously offered us the use of their place. The money generated from the sale of these tickets and our paper, in which some of the youngsters wrote stories and poems, enabled us to expand our excursions into areas that were both enjoyable and educational. We went to museums and the Monnaie, the famous opera house where the youngsters were introduced to the beauty of *Carmen* and *La Traviata*. This activity filled me with a great sense of satisfaction, though it left little time to get ready for the coming school year.

I had been given a small starting salary, which I handed over to my parents, who were still having a hard time making ends meet. My father's new position, though certainly an improvement over the Swiss job, had not turned out as we had hoped. He had been given a small territory in a mostly rural area and the storeowners were slow in trying a new firm.

One day my boss called me into her office. She wanted to know what my plans were. I told her about our failed attempt to secure the American visa and our hope that we would get a second chance before long. As to my immediate future, I was not sure what to do. I was confident though that we would leave Europe by the end of the year and was reluctant to go back to school for another term.

"Let me know what you decide," she told me. "I will have a place for you, if you want it."

After discussing it with my parents at great length, I decided to accept the offer of becoming a full-time employee. To say that I did not have any misgivings would be an understatement. I fully recognized that those years were crucial to my education, but I hoped to catch up with lost time once we arrived in America.

Nineteen thirty-eight turned out to be a watershed year. The year had seen the annexation of Austria by Hitler, the so-called Anschluss, an ominous indication of the Nazis' plan to dominate Europe. In the fall, the world came close to war once again when Neville Chamberlain, England's prime minister, and Edouard Daladier of France caved in at Munich by ceding the Sudetenland, part of Czechoslovakia, to Germany. Thus, a small valiant people were sacrificed to avert a war, in the hope of having satisfied Hitler's insatiable quest for expansion. Those were the days when we were all terrified at the thought that war was about to explode and that little Belgium would present no barrier to a German assault.

When Chamberlain returned to London from Berchtesgarden, the Fuehrer's headquarters where that appeasement disaster had taken place, and proudly announced "Peace in our time," we too were relieved, although it was clear to us that all that had been gained was some time to prepare for the inevitable.

The year ended with a dramatic event that foreshadowed the horrors of things to come: the burning of synagogues throughout Germany and Austria and the destruction of Jewish-owned store fronts known as Kristallnacht, "The Night of the Broken Glass." Scores of Jews were killed, thousands were arrested and sent to concentration camps. Fire brigades, following official orders, let the torched synagogues and stores burn, but protected adjacent Aryan property. The catalyst had been the assassination of the German attaché at the embassy in Paris, Ernst Vom Rath, by a seventeen-year-old Jewish boy, Hershel Grynszpan, who lived in Paris with his uncle and who had been driven to that attack after learning his parents had been deported to Poland.

It was the opportunity for the Nazis to put some of their nefarious plans into action. A precedent had been established with that pogrom. There were, however, no sudden moves by any country, including the United States, to open their borders. As Joseph Goebbels, the Nazi propaganda minister remarked, "It looks as if the rest of the world does not want the chosen people either."

At the committee, there was now a frantic effort on the way to find asylum for as many refugees as possible, before the doors would be closed to them. To the everlasting shame of the free world, only a handful of countries agreed to accept a small number of them.

After only a month on my job, I received a raise, which made me very happy. I decided not to tell my parents. I wanted to save that unexpected windfall. I was certain the day would come when we would need it. In order to force myself not to touch that extra cash, I exchanged the francs for one U.S. dollar every week. The steady accumulation of these green backs filled me with great pride, though it was not easy to keep this a secret.

I also bought some books published by the Berlitz School and started to teach myself English. That way, I felt, I did not completely give up on my education.

Shortly before my sixteenth birthday, I fell in love with a very pretty girl who had joined the club. Ilse was from Cologne and had a younger sister. Her parents planned to immigrate to Canada. Her father had been a livestock dealer, and since the Canadian government was anxious to accept refugees with a background in agriculture, they stood an excellent chance of obtaining the entrance permit. Ilse was fourteen years old and had dazzling blue eyes, a scrubbed look that radiated good health, and a mischievous smile.

There is something very special about that first love and for a while we were able to forget the grim world around us. Just weeks before September 1, 1939, when German armies entered Poland, Ilse and her family left for Canada. I walked the streets of Brussels with a heavy heart. "We will meet again, when I come to the States," I promised. Ah, the wonderful illusions of youth!

Meanwhile, our own efforts to secure that precious visa now seemed doomed. Hitler, having previously neutralized the Soviet Union by signing a non-aggression pact—thus guaranteeing their cooperation and offering them the eastern part of a divided Poland—now unleashed his "blitzkrieg" against a vastly inferior enemy. On the third of September, France and Great Britain declared war, in compliance with their promise to come to Poland's rescue if it was attacked.

We used to eat our main meal at a small pension run by a friend of ours on the second floor of an office building on Boulevard Adolphe Max, in the center of Brussels. Lina Abramovitsch was a jolly, smartly dressed woman, always in good spirits, who served delicious meals at a very low price to a handful of guests, mostly Jewish students from Germany, Austria and Rumania. It turned out a very good deal for us, as we would often share our meals between ourselves.

A large map of Poland had been pinned to the kitchen wall of Lina's pension. Every day we marked in red the advance of the German Wehrmacht and our spirits would sink as we realized that the war against the Germans could not last long on that front. The winter brought the beginning of the *drôle de guerre,* "the phony war," as the near total inactivity on the western front was called. French and German soldiers were facing each other along heavy fortifications for days, without as much as firing a shot.

Soon that peculiar period ended, when German troops invaded Denmark and Norway in April of 1940. While little Denmark offered only token resistance, Norway fought on with a fierce determination, but in the end was no match for the German army. We were now sure that spring would bring the long awaited confrontation in the west.

On April 15, we received a registered letter from the American consulate in Antwerp. We opened it with great trepidation, only to burst out in a long cheer. It was the invitation to pick up the precious visa!

The scheduled appointment was for May 14.

Chapter Three

War Comes to the West

On May 10, 1940, around six o'clock in the morning, I was awakened by the sound of planes above the city and the intermittent staccato of anti-aircraft fire. I walked to the window. The sky was filled with small black crosses as far as the eye could see. Occasionally white clouds reached out to the attacking Stukas, but seemed to fall short of their target. Sirens filled the air and bombs were bursting at regular intervals. In the distance I saw black smoke rising from the city below.

It was my seventeenth birthday.

"Happy birthday, my son," my mother said, embracing me. "It is one you will always remember." She started to cry.

"Let's hope we will survive what is ahead of us," my father said. Then he added, "Fortunately we have the French and the British to come to our rescue."

I shook my head. "I am afraid we are in for a very tough battle."

After about twenty minutes the sirens signaled the end of the raid. Over the protest of my parents, I decided to go outside to find out the extent of the damage. The streets were filled with people scurrying around as if in shock, trying to come to grips with the fact that their small country had now been engulfed in war. There was surprisingly little damage in our neighborhood.

When I came to Avenue Louise, an exclusive area ten minutes from us, I saw a number of buildings badly damaged. One house had its entire front torn away, as if cut by a giant knife. A bed was dangling precariously from a second floor, ready to crash into the street below at any moment. I counted four houses that were engulfed in heavy smoke. Firefighters worked feverishly to divert the spread of the flames. Ambulance sirens filled the air. On a street corner, people had gathered around a woman who was lying motionless on a stretcher while medics were trying to resuscitate her.

I decided to return to our place. In spite of the great number of planes, it appeared that the city, at least in the areas I had seen, had suffered less damage than I expected. Still, this was only the first strike, and I was convinced that soon others would follow.

I told my parents that we should pack and get out of the city as fast as possible. The logical place was Paris, some three hundred kilometers from Brussels, where I was certain we would be safe, protected by that "Grande Armée." My father disagreed.

"The French and British will stop them," he sounded surprisingly optimistic. Let's wait another day."

We dressed and went to see Lina at her restaurant. A number of the regulars had arrived, in spite of the early morning hour. We huddled around the radio, listening to King Leopold addressing the nation, exhorting the people to fight the enemy together with our allies and promising victory. We all decided to wait another day to see how the military situation was going to develop.

Throughout the day, detachments of French soldiers with their tanks and heavy artillery passed through the city, and were greeted with wild applause by the crowds lining the sidewalks. In the afternoon, the British, with their distinctive helmets, followed. Our spirits lifted. We were sure that they would soon push back the Germans.

Towards evening, news came from the front that heavy fighting had broken out along the Meuse River. Rumors circulated that German paratroopers had secured a beachhead on the river's west bank.

The next morning a smaller number of planes appeared over the city. The piercing sound of the Stukas as they dove towards their targets, unloading their deadly cargo, was spine-chilling. As we watched, mesmerized from our bedroom window, the phone rang. It was Lina who asked us to come over at once.

On the way to her, we saw French and British soldiers coming back from the front, some on foot, others in trucks, now moving in the opposite direction, towards the French border. Apparently, the Germans had not been stopped, but had in fact broken through the Allied lines and were headed straight in our direction. By launching an all-out massive drive through the Netherlands, Belgium and Luxembourg, they had by-passed the famous Maginot Line, the "impregnable fortress" along the Western front.

We found Lina and her family sitting around the dining room table studying a large map. "We have decided to take the early train for Paris tomorrow morning," Lina's husband announced. "We suggest you do the same."

The handwriting was on the wall. Even if the Allies were able to eventually turn the tide, the possibility of the Germans overrunning Brussels in the next few days was more than likely. We were determined not to fall into their hands.

The following day, May 13, in the very early morning hours and just three days after the German onslaught, we were on our way to the station where we met our friends and their children. We managed to board the last train leaving for Paris.

Because we had been among the very first to arrive at the station, when the city was still shrouded in darkness, we were able to secure three seats. So had our friends in the compartment next to us. Looking out the window we realized how fortunate we had been, as the platform was soon swamped by hundreds of desperate men, women and children weighed down with suitcases and parcels, frantically pushing and shoving in their attempt to board the train. The gendarmes stationed there to keep order were unable to control what threatened to turn into a stampede.

Certain disaster was avoided when the stationmaster finally gave the departure signal and the train started to move slowly, leaving behind the many whose hopes to escape that imminent threat had vanished. There seemed not an inch of space left on that train. Most of the travelers with seats had children on their laps. The less fortunate were standing in the aisles with barely any breathing room.

"We should be in Paris in about six hours," I said, turning to my father. "I sure hope there won't be any delay, or else we could be in for some trouble." We had made it on to the train, but I was still apprehensive.

Over the next few hours the train roared through the countryside, without slowing down. I stepped outside our compartment and tried to edge up to a window, hoping to catch a road sign that would identify the locality we were passing. Glancing at my watch, I realized that we had traveled almost three hours and should be past the halfway mark to Paris.

A man standing next to me and looking up at the sky, started to shake his head while mumbling to himself. Turning toward me, he said in an angry voice, "I don't know where this train is going, but it sure as hell ain't Paris."

"What makes you say that?" I asked.

"For one thing, we are moving into a northwestern direction instead of a southwestern one. This train's headed for the coast of Normandy."

"How can that be?" I asked incredulously. "We aren't going to England, are we?"

The man just kept on shaking his head.

The train had made no stops, nor was there a conductor in sight. The lines in front of the toilets were getting longer, while the tempers of the passengers got shorter. Mothers with crying babies on their arms were pushing through the lines, trying to reach the water faucet.

My father motioned me back into the compartment. "I am sure the train will stop soon and everybody will be able to get water. In the meantime, sit down if you want to keep your seat." My mother peeled an apple I had in my backpack and offered it to me. A woman sitting next to me with a small boy on her lap, looked at me longingly. I handed the apple to her. She thanked me and gave it to the child.

All through the night the train kept at the same speed, never stopping. Gradually everybody became aware that something was very wrong. People started to yell, clamoring for the conductor. One of the men pointed to the emergency brake, but nobody dared to pull it. Around midnight the train came to a sudden stop, causing some of the passengers to collide with each other.

I looked out of the window, but was only able to discern a barely lit platform where a number of soldiers, with side arms, were posted every twenty feet.

A voice came over the loudspeaker; "This train has been rerouted for safety reasons. It will not go to Paris. You will not be allowed to get off until the final destination, which is in the South. At the next stop there will be water available. Do not attempt to leave the train or stop it or you will be arrested."

Within seconds the train started to move again, rapidly gaining top speed. An older man brandishing his cane began to scream, demanding to be let out. A few passengers tried to organize the lines for the bathroom and asked other passengers who had brought provisions on the trip to give some of the food and drinks to the children.

I was getting very tired, but hard as I tried it was impossible to take a nap, not even for a few minutes, with that unending screaming and yelling filling the air. In the morning a foul odor coming from the overstuffed toilets, where the flushing system had long since ceased to function, pervaded every compartment and added to the misery of the travelers on this "ghost train to nowhere."

Soon tempers flared. Two men, in the compartment next to ours exchanged insults that lead to a fistfight. It took all the efforts of some of the more level heads among us to break up the brawl.

When the sun came up, I tried to make out some of the signs as the train raced through one station after the other. We were apparently traveling somewhere along the Atlantic Coast, and according to one passenger who knew the region, close to Nantes. The promised stop never took place.

The morning of the third day, our nightmare finally came to an end. The train stopped at a place called Revel. It turned out to be a small town near

Toulouse, in the department of Haute-Garonne. We had landed in the south of France. Disheveled, having been without water for nearly three days and in dire need of changing clothes, we couldn't wait to get off that ill-fated train.

A number of gendarmes were lined up along the platform. Using a foghorn, one of them admonished us to stay put until the order to disembark was given. After a few minutes, we started to pour out of the train and take our first whiff of fresh air in thirty-six hours. We were directed toward the waiting room where we were given numbers corresponding to buses lined up in front of the station. Women in Red Cross uniforms were handing out water bottles, bread and fruit to the nearly starved passengers. My mother, who suffered from chronic arthritis, could only walk with my father's help.

A short bus ride brought us to a soccer field where a large tent had been erected. Police officers were sitting behind tables that had signs posted with letters of the alphabet. We were told to line up according to our last name. After examining our identification cards carefully, the officers handed us vouchers with the name and address of a French family who had volunteered to provide shelter and food and would receive a payment from the local authorities for every refugee they took in.

We were directed to a narrow, cobble-stoned street where we located our host's residence, a small two-story building. Though it obviously was a rather old house, it seemed in good condition. From the second story balcony, red gardenias in flowerpots were a welcome sight.

Madame Bouchard turned out to be a plump, short woman in a red-checkered blouse and a black skirt. She motioned us into her house. She took the voucher, put it in her purse, and asked us to sit down on a velour couch in what appeared to be a combination of foyer and kitchen. Pointing to a short man in his fifties, who was snoring in a lounge chair, she said, "This is Monsieur Bouchard, my husband." Lowering her voice she added, "He carries a bag around his waist. He cannot pee, *le pauvre*." It was a rather startling introduction.

After offering us a glass of wine and some grapes, Madame Bouchard proceeded to show us a small room with a large bed. "This is for you and your wife," she said addressing my father. "You will sleep here," she said, motioning me to the adjacent room, not much larger than a wall closet. With that she pulled down a Murphy bed from the wall. I thanked her and told her this would do just fine.

It was truly amazing how easily we managed to fit into our new environment. While we were confined to just a room and a closet, Madame Bouchard tried her best to make our stay comfortable. It seemed to us that she was actually enjoying the change in what was apparently a rather dreary existence.

My mother helped around the house, cleaning and working in the kitchen, while my father and I took turns in bringing wood logs from a shed to feed the stove, saving the precious coal supply.

Madame Bouchard confided in us, divulging what surely were pent-up feelings of unhappiness about her daughter-in-law who, she told us, had consorted with men ever since her son Antoine had been called into the army six months earlier. *"Elle est une putain,* she is a whore," she kept telling us.

There was also a younger daughter in the house, Yvonne, aged fifteen, who had an enormous bosom that she flaunted with great delight. Since school was out, she just lounged around all day. Her room was in the attic above the kitchen. On the second night, she came down the stairs, slipped into the closet and cuddled next to me. When I awoke, rather startled, she took my hand and put it on her right breast, which she had uncovered. For a moment I was struggling between my first impulse to gratefully accept what she so graciously offered and the fear of the consequences that would surely lead to our being expelled from this place. I decided to gently push her away, telling her that it was late and that she must go back to her room at once. Needless to say, that it was not an easy decision. I felt that there was always the possibility of another and better occasion.

That occasion, however, would not present itself, as Yvonne, according to Madame Bouchard, having decided to spend some time with her cousin in Avignon, departed the following day.

We heard from some of the other refugees that not all hosts were as hospitable as the Bouchards. There had been incidents of antisemitic outbursts and only the fact that they were paid well seemed to have swayed some of the reluctant hosts to keep their guests.

The news from the front was sparse. What transpired was not good. The Germans, it seemed, had abandoned a direct frontal assault on Paris and instead, were pushing toward Dunkirk on the coast, where British troops were now engaged in a fierce battle.

Ten days after our arrival in Revel, an announcement was posted at the *mairie,* the town hall, instructing all men between the ages of eighteen and forty-five who were citizens of a country allied with France to immediately register for military service. This would include the majority of the refugees, who were carrying passports from Belgium, Holland, Luxembourg and Poland. My father and I let out a sigh of relief, as he was forty-six years old and I had just turned seventeen a few weeks earlier. We still had to appear in person to receive the official exemption paper.

A surly clerk went through my father's papers in a hurry and dismissed him with a wave of his hand. He took an unduly long time inspecting my identification card. Finally, he looked up. "You'll do fine," he said stamping a printed form. "Present yourself tomorrow morning at 8:00 a.m. at the train station with this paper. Your destination is the town of Bressuire, the headquarters of the Polish army in France."

For a moment I was speechless. Then I said, "Sir, I am only seventeen and I am exempt."

"Not in my book, you aren't," he said, raising his voice. "We have our French boys who are volunteering at seventeen to fight the Boche. It won't hurt you to do something for the country that took you in."

My father tried to intercede on my behalf, but the clerk ordered him to shut up or he would face arrest. "Take it up with the Polish authorities," he told me. "Just make sure to be there tomorrow morning!"

My father's family had come to Germany from Poland when he was only two years old, but he never applied for German citizenship. As a result, we all had Polish passports, even I who was born in Frankfurt.

When my mother heard the news, she became very upset. "Don't worry," I told her, "the war may be over soon and I'll be back in no time." Actually, I was not totally disappointed at the prospect of going into the army. At seventeen, I saw this as an adventure and did not give the potential dangers much thought.

The next morning, I was at the station along with some five hundred men, most of them Jewish and apparently all Polish citizens. I was wearing a light gray wool suit, the only one I owned and much too heavy for the sweltering heat, but I could not possibly arrive at headquarters dressed in shorts.

My mother had filled my backpack with underwear, a couple of shirts and socks. At the last minute, she added a can of sweetened condensed milk she had saved. "You will need this," she said. "It is very nutritious. Save it to supplement your army rations."

I promised her I would, but after three hours on that train I opened the can and gorged myself. I then carefully wrapped the half empty can in a newspaper before stuffing it into my backpack. Eight hours later, we finally arrived at our destination. I looked out the window.

Six Polish officers were standing at the ramp, dressed in black uniforms, wearing funny looking slanted caps and watching the arrival of the new recruits in grim silence. One of them started to give orders in Polish, which evidently was understood by most of the recruits as they swiftly lined up with their parcels. The man to my left gave me a brief translation after the next order was issued. "He wants us to open all bags and parcels, so he can check their contents," he told me.

"What for?" I asked.

"For weapons," he replied.

"Weapons?" I said, "Why in the world would we bring weapons to an army post? What are they afraid of?"

He shook his head, "I have no idea."

I put my backpack down. The officer closest to me motioned me to hurry up. He obviously was not satisfied with the speed I followed his order. Angrily, he grabbed my bag, tore the strings open, and put his hand in the bag. Then he let out a scream. He had pulled out the can of condensed milk, from which the paper had dropped, causing the gooey liquid to spill all over his uniform. What followed next, was, I suppose, a torrent of Polish curses; his face was red and flushed and he looked as if he was about to have a stroke. Since I did not understand a word, I kept on shrugging my shoulders and managed an apologetic smile.

The men who had witnessed the mishap had a hard time not to burst out laughing but thought the better of it, given the likely consequences. I on the other hand, was fully prepared to be, if not shot on the spot, at least court-martialed.

While the officer was busy soaking up the mess with a handkerchief, still ranting and raving, another motioned us toward the station exit. After marching through the center of town, where a few civilians watched us with indifference, we arrived at our destination.

It turned out to be the local jail. According to David, our translator, there were no quarters ready for the new recruits of the Polish army. Since the jail was only occupied by a couple of drunkards, blissfully unaware of France's growing predicament, it seemed the ideal place.

I had an entire cell to myself. The furnishings consisted of a narrow cot with a flimsy mattress and a tiny table. In the corner I detected a hole in the ground that I assumed served as a toilet.

"They have no uniforms for us," my friend explained. Then he added, "and no weapons either." Exactly what we were supposed to do here was a puzzle.

That question, however, was answered the following morning after roll call. A corporal handed out shovels and ordered us to dig trenches. "We are supposed to slow down the advancing German tanks," David explained with a straight face.

The only one I knew among the recruits from Revel was Julien, a lanky, good- natured fellow a year older than I. We decided to stick close together.

Two days later, a sergeant who spoke some French informed me I had been recruited by mistake, since I was only seventeen years old. "You are free to go back home," he said. When I asked him how I was to accomplish this, he shrugged his shoulders and walked away.

With the cannon thunder getting closer and no way for me to leave, I decided to go "on strike." Since I should not have been sent here in the first place, I felt that I did not have to dig trenches in that miserable heat. I stayed on my cot and skipped roll call. I had found a few empty medicine bottles. When the Lieutenant came to inspect the place, he started to scream in Polish, obviously furious that I was still in my cell. "*Je suis malade,* I am sick," I moaned in my most convincing voice, pointing to the medicine bottles. After a while, he just walked out.

The next morning, I woke up to an eerie silence. On the outside, a number of men were huddled, talking in low voices. Julien appeared. "Our officers and soldiers have flown the coupe," he said. "There is not one of them left."

David filled in the gaps. The Polish detachment had been given orders to evacuate Bressuire and reach the port of Bordeaux, where they were to board a British war ship leaving for England. They had pulled out at dawn in a few army trucks and cars.

"What about us?" David had asked one of the officers.

"Just start walking back to where you came from," the officer told him before jumping into his car.

I shook my head in disbelief. "Is he crazy? Walking five hundred kilometers with the Germans in hot pursuit does not strike me as a great idea!"

Most recruits seemed to think it was, as they promptly began marching, braving the grueling sun on that dusty highway.

The road was packed with all kinds of vehicles rushing in a southern direction, in the hope of out-racing the German army. Most of them were loaded with suitcases and household items, including one car that had a bed strapped to its roof. I spotted a number of French officers in full uniform, who evidently had decided on their own that the war was over.

"Let them all go," I told Julien. "Nobody will stop for hundreds of men marching together, but we may have a chance if they see just the two of us trying to thumb a ride." We sat down along a road marker, our bundles next to us. Soon the column disappeared in the distance.

A number of vehicles passed us without stopping. Then we saw a small red convertible. Two young girls, their hair blowing in the wind, were the only occupants. We waved frantically and the car came to a screeching halt. After we had told them of our dilemma, they pointed to a very narrow back seat, partially filled with suitcases. Julien squeezed into the empty spot and motioned me to sit on his lap. The girls were first year students at the Sorbonne in Paris and on their way home to Limoges, a town in the general direction of our destination. While we would still have to cover a good distance before reaching Revel, it certainly was a tremendous help. In just minutes we passed our comrades.

While the ride was not very comfortable, especially for Julien, we had a rather good time, talking to the girls and exchanging stories. They found my encounter with that Polish officer hilarious. A couple of hours later, at the entrance of Limoges, the girls let us off and wished us good luck.

We were looking for a place to buy a few provisions, when suddenly the sirens started to wail. A small cluster of planes appeared in the sky and abruptly went into a diving mode, emitting a howling sound while strafing the ground with their machine guns. We jumped into one of the ditches that must have been dug recently as a few shovels were still piled on the ground.

After the sirens announced the end of the alarm, we ventured out and surveyed the area. Two trucks, riddled with bullets, were on fire, but we did not see any occupants. A woman walking along the road was cradling a child in her arms and seemed lost.

Out of nowhere, two gendarmes appeared, approaching us in a threatening way. "*Vos papiers*," one of them said in a stern voice. We handed him our papers identifying us as Allied Polish conscripts. The two seemed to have some doubts.

"We had a number of 'fifth column' individuals in civilian clothes dropped by German planes behind the French lines, to guide the advancing German troops," the other said. Our assurances that we were loyal soldiers caught in the general retreat fell on deaf ears. They escorted us to a nearby police station, where an officer, after scrutinizing our papers for a long time, finally concluded that we were telling the truth and let us go.

We were fortunate to get another lift in the direction of Bordeaux. We arrived in the early evening, just when the Luftwaffe was descending on a flotilla assembled in the harbor and ready to sail for England. After the planes had turned back, meeting a rather strong barrage of anti-aircraft batteries, we entertained for a fleeting moment the thought of making it to England. In the end, we decided to go back to Revel and our parents.

"Maybe the German advance will be stopped at some point," Julien ventured, without much conviction.

It was getting dark. We walked to the railroad station and hopped on a train we found out was going to Toulouse, just fifty kilometers from Revel. In Toulouse, we flagged down a truck that made deliveries in the area. Luck was with us as the driver told us that Revel was on his route.

We were the first ones back in town and received a hero's welcome. My parents and Julien's were deliriously happy to see us safe and sound.

Within days the war came to an end. The collapse of France caught most Frenchmen by surprise. Somehow they had hoped for a miracle, but the

French army was no match for the German Panzers, supported by hundreds of planes that dominated the sky. When Hitler's troops marched down the Champs Élysées, the people of Paris watched in silence, their hearts broken.

Some members of the French government took refuge in North Africa, while General Charles De Gaulle, an outspoken officer who refused to enter into any peace negotiations with the Nazis, went to London with a small nucleus of officers to continue the fight.

The British managed to retreat to the port of Dunkirk and board the ships waiting to take them back to England, saving most of the corps though nearly all of the equipment stayed behind.

On June 22, the new French government formed at Vichy under the leadership of Marshal Philippe Pétain, the hero of Verdun in World War I, signed an armistice with the victorious Germans.

Chapter Four

Camp Agde

France was now divided into two parts. The entire north with Paris and all of the Atlantic coast was under German military command. The southern half, including the areas bordering Switzerland and Italy, the Mediterranean coast, except for an Italian enclave, and large population centers such as Lyon, Marseille, and Toulouse were under the sovereignty of the Pétain government. The new capital was Vichy, a famous spa in the center of the country. While this would lend a quasi-independence to "La Nouvelle France," it was clear that all the important decisions would come from the German headquarters in Paris. Still, we were relieved when we became aware of these demarcation zones. We hoped that living in the Unoccupied Zone would protect us from the iron grip of the occupier in the north.

On October 3, 1940, three months after signing the armistice, the Vichy government decreed the "Statut des Juifs," an ordinance regulating the lives of both French and foreign Jews, putting severe limitations on what jobs would be open to them. French Jews were barred from public service, the armed forces, teaching, journalism, theatre, radio and cinema, among other fields.

A week later a notice was posted at city hall, instructing all foreigners to report at once to the police station. My parents and I were among the 1,200 refugees assembled that morning, hearing the mayor announce our relocation to the town of Agde, a port on the Mediterranean. We would be assigned to barracks formerly used to house members of the Spanish Republican Army who had fled to France in 1937 after their defeat by Franco. Abandoned for several years, this camp would now be the home of a new crop of refugees. On the day of our departure, we stood in line at the train station, wondering what was next in store for us.

The mere introduction of the word "camp" could not help but fill us with a deep sense of apprehension. We, who had witnessed the creation of Dachau and Buchenwald, knew that from this moment on our freedom would be taken from us. No rationalizing about the Republic that had given shelter to so many victims of Hitler's persecution during the thirties could lift that feeling of foreboding. This much was certain: the Jews would be the first to pay the price of France's defeat.

We arrived at our destination in the late afternoon. Buses were lined up to bring us to the campgrounds. The clear blue waters shimmering in the warm sun and the white beaches stretching for miles were a welcome sight, until we saw infinite rows of ramshackle, wooden charcoal gray barracks standing fifteen feet apart with several guard houses towering over them and ringed by eight-foot-high barbed wire. No trees surrounded the structures and barely a few tufts of grass were visible.

The commandant, a tall, middle-aged man in a slightly shopworn uniform was accompanied by several other officers. He told us that this was an internment camp and that the men were to be separated from the women and children who had their own barracks. A sergeant, sitting at a makeshift desk, started to process the crowd at an excruciatingly slow pace. My mother opened her suitcase and handed me my clothes, since I would be lodged with my father. We embraced and went in different directions, convinced that we would meet the following day, once the admission process was completed.

Our barracks were seventy-five feet long and twenty feet wide. Two rows of double-decked wooden planks on either side were covered with a thin layer of straw. It was a hot day. The damp, musty straw, on which cockroaches were crawling, filled the air with a putrid smell. My father and I were assigned the upper berth. Because there were one hundred men squeezed into each building, the individual space was no more than two feet wide.

In the morning, we lined up for roll call. We were given our daily ration of bread laced with sawdust to stretch the meager wheat content, a quarter loaf per person, and were admonished to keep it in a secure place, preferably dangling from a rope tied between the top of two bunks so that the rats would not get to it. We found out, much to our dismay, that this precaution was not very successful, as we were left with just half of our ration. Apparently the rats were skilled at rope walking.

There were no organized activities of any kind. The guards left us to our own devices. Some volunteered for kitchen duty. Others started to get rid of that grime that covered nearly everything.

A few days after our arrival we had torrential rains that transformed the swampy grounds around the barracks into a lake. We had to lay down wooden boards to reach the outdoor latrines, which consisted of a row of holes in the ground with two slabs of cement to stand on. There were no dividers. Some of the latrines had overflowed and soon the entire area was transformed into a giant sewer, serving as a breeding ground for mosquitoes, while inside the barracks we had to fight the onslaught of lice and fleas. We found out that the condition on the women's side was even worse, as they had to relieve themselves in trenches.

It became clear to us that the authorities had been totally unprepared to receive the new occupants. After the rains we tried to fix a number of leaky roofs with makeshift tools. Our complaints to the commandant fell on deaf ears.

We had been interned for several weeks when we were allowed to visit the women's compound. My mother was happy to see us. She introduced us to the other women who shared the quarters with her. Their sleeping facilities were better than ours. They had individual bunk beds with sufficient straw and covered with a wool blanket. The smaller children had to share their space with another child. My mother told us that her blanket had reeked from filth and that she had to wash and scrub it for a long time before she felt ready to sleep on it.

After the visit of a rabbi from a nearby town, conditions improved somewhat. He had food packages and clothing sent in, as well as badly needed medicines. Our days became more structured. The women were given uniforms to launder and repair while the men with special skills did carpentry and electrical work. Some of the needed tools had been donated by local merchants. My father, who was fluent in three languages, was helping in the commandant's office, keeping records and translating letters some of the inmates had received from relatives in America. He convinced the commandant to let him contact the American consulate in Marseille to initiate steps that would lead to obtaining an entrance visa for them.

The main prerequisite was an affidavit by a relative, guaranteeing that the new immigrant would not become a burden to the state. My father's efforts paid off, as the consul was helpful in expediting these applications. He further wrote to some Jewish organizations, approached churches and appealed to the authorities in Beziers, the site of the prefecture, asking for warm clothes for the approaching winter, special food for babies, toys for the young children and schoolbooks for the older ones.

The commandant was very much impressed with my father's work. His attitude changed. Whereas before he was rather aloof and seemed not at all pleased with his assignment, he now became gradually friendlier and took an interest in the lives of the refugees in his charge.

One night we awoke to the sound of screams coming from the women's compound. Rushing outside, we saw flames shooting sky high, engulfing a number of structures. Heavy smoke filled the air. Women and children, screaming for help, were trying to reach our barracks. I ran as fast as I could to get to my mother's side, but was stopped by guards who had formed a cordon around the burning structures and were passing buckets of water, trying to contain the flames. I was able to slip through and reached my mother's building. Thick billows of black smoke made it hard to see anything. I called out her name and finally found her slumped to the floor, but conscious. The fire, it seemed, had started in the adjacent barrack, but had not yet reached hers. I pulled her out and led her to our side. The soldiers were finally able to confine the flames to just two structures that burned to the ground.

My mother wound up in the infirmary, suffering from smoke inhalation and minor abrasions. Fortunately, she would recover within days. Two women had serious burns and had to be rushed to the hospital at Beziers. The others were treated in the infirmary.

Winter arrived with vengeance. An icy wind from the sea blew through the poorly heated barracks. Two kerosene ovens at either end were not enough to provide sufficient heat for hundred inmates. We all went to bed in whatever we owned to keep warm. It was, we were told, the coldest winter in years. My father sent urgent messages to relief organizations, among them the American Jewish Joint Distribution Committee, asking them to provide badly needed additional wool blankets and warm clothing, especially for the children. The commandant made my father the official spokesman for the 1,200 refugees whose confidence he had earned through his unrelenting efforts on their behalf.

With the severe weather the hygienic conditions in the camp worsened. Cases of dysentery and the flu started to take a toll among the elderly. A team of medical workers sent from the town of Agde, tried their best to stem what threatened to become an epidemic, but a number of the elderly and two infants died that winter.

I too had caught the flu. Shuddering from cold and running a high fever, I was brought to the infirmary. Few antibiotics were available and nearly all of them reserved for the children. With the little money my father had left, he was able to buy a small bottle of brandy from one of the guards. Unaccustomed as I was to liquor, this remedy turned out to be a lifesaver. I got better within a week.

Spring came not a moment too soon.

All throughout the next few months, we followed the war that raged in North Africa, where Germany's General Rommel was pushing the British across Libya and into Egypt.

On June 22, Germany, breaking its non-aggression pact with the Soviet Union, launched an all-out assault on Russia called "Operation Barbarossa." The Germans were now immersed in a two-front war. We hoped that this turn of events would prove fatal to the Nazis. Unfortunately, the news from the front during the first few weeks of battle was anything but encouraging. The German armies were overrunning Soviet positions everywhere, moving deeply into their territory.

In the early days of August, the commandant informed my father that the camp was going to be closed. All inmates were to be placed in nearby communities and work assignments given to all able-bodied men.

"This will be a great improvement over camp life," he said. He then asked my father to help him prepare the transfer. He pulled out a map of the region and pointed to a small town near Valence. Aubenas, he explained, is a fortress town, dating back to the Romans. "It is a lovely place," he added, "with a castle, surrounded by vineyards and densely wooded areas. I visited that town last year. I believe it would be a good place for you and your family to wait out the war."

On August 15, together with another Jewish family, we arrived at our new destination with some apprehension, but also with hopes that things would look up from here on. Above all, we would finally leave that camp and all its misery behind.

Chapter Five

Aubenas

Aubenas turned out as the major had described. Winding cobblestone streets led to the main town square, which was filled with stalls of flowers and carts loaded with fruit brought in from the surrounding farms. Towering above the town stood a Gothic castle dating back to the twelfth century, adorned with turrets and colorful tiles. A magnificent golden cupola, glittering in the sunlight, covered the church in the center of the town. Most stores displayed brightly painted signs, indicating a bakery, a shoemaker and two butcher shops—one selling regular meat and the other, the less expensive but quite popular horse meat.

We had been given the address of a house located at the bottom of a hilly street. Two sisters, Genevieve and Giselle Martin had offered to rent us a room on the second floor of the place they shared with their eighty-five-year-old mother. The rent was reasonable and was paid for by a Jewish organization that had been working with the local authorities. This was intended as a temporary assistance to cover our rent and food expenses until my father and I started to receive our first wages.

Shortly after our arrival, I was assigned to a vineyard where they strapped a large wooden basket to my back. I was instructed to walk along the vines, heavy with grapes ready to be picked. At least two dozen women, their hair covered with colorful scarves, were working at full speed, cutting the fruit and throwing the bunches into my basket.

After a while, the load became unbearable heavy, but I was determined to keep going until I reached a large vat, into which I was supposed to pour the contents, not an easy feat to accomplish without losing my balance. A group of women were stomping on the grapes with their bare feet, a process that would eventually lead to that bottle of wine on a Frenchman's dinner table.

My father had the misfortune to be sent to a sawmill a couple of miles from our residence. He was paired with a husky, burly man in his twenties to cut down trees with an enormous saw. The young man took great delight in pulling that saw with all his strength, propelling my father forward and causing him to stumble and lose his grip. My father was a slim, short man who had never done anything close to that kind of work; he was mercilessly taunted by the other workers, who used some of the vilest antisemitic expletives. Unfortunately, neither he nor I had any choice in the type of work we had been asked to perform.

At night my father would come home from this ordeal, shuffling along, barely able to walk and stopping frequently on the way. Sometimes when I got home before he did, I watched him from our window. My heart ached and I felt terrible seeing him so broken in body and spirit.

This, for sure, was not the improvement the major had promised us. I contacted the Jewish organization that had been very helpful before. They promised to make inquiries about other possible jobs, but they were not successful.

The pay we received was barely sufficient to take care of the rent and a minimum of food. My mother had made the acquaintance of a few women who had complained that they were unable to find any shoes because of a dire shortage of leather. She got hold of some raffia, a cheap straw-like material. My father and I, after our strenuous day, were put to work, transforming these strings into braids, employing a method similar to basket weaving. My mother, using a very large needle, then sewed them together, a tedious and painful procedure that left sores and blisters on her fingers. Creating a base that became a sole, she then sewed cotton material that had been supplied by the women to that sole and a solid, very usable pair of slippers was created. My mother's ingenuity thus brought in some badly needed extra money.

Both of my parents were avid smokers. Their allocated rations proved totally inadequate and we resorted to bartering our wine rations for tobacco ones.

Our two landladies treated us with kindness, slipping us a few eggs, or an extra ration of butter during the month. In turn, I made myself useful, helping them in their yard on weekends.

The winter was even harsher than the one we had experienced in the camp. We gathered wood in the nearby forest to stretch the meager coal ration we had been given. Our stove did not provide much heat and we went to bed bundled in heavy clothes, a stark reminder of our recent camp days. The mill was closed and there was no work at the vineyard.

I started visiting the local library, searching for books that would help me further my education. One afternoon, while I was piling up books on my desk, a nicely dressed woman sat down next to me. We soon engaged in conversation about modern literature and world history and she apparently enjoyed our exchange of ideas.

She told me that she had a sixteen-year-old son who needed help with his homework. Would I be interested in tutoring him? I was only too happy to accept that unexpected offer. Considering that I had less of a formal education than my prospective pupil—a fact I did not volunteer—this was indeed a challenge, but I managed to get through each session successfully by studying the planned lesson the day before I was to meet him. Jean-Pierre did very well on his tests and his grateful mother gave me an extra bonus, which helped us greatly during that harsh winter.

In the spring, I met Danielle. She was the baker's daughter and she had recently started working for her father after school, waiting on customers and helping with deliveries. When I first saw her, I was struck by her beautiful dark eyes, rosy cheeks, and the friendly smile with which she greeted me. Her hair was hidden under a white bonnet, with some of the shiny brown strands managing to stick out. When I came into the bakery with my bread ration stamps, we engaged in what the French call *badiner,* a harmless form of pleasant chatter.

One day, as I was paying her for my loaf, I noticed her putting back the ration stamps into the bag she had just wrapped. I was about to point out the mistake to her when she ever so slightly shook her head. It was the beginning of our never running out of bread.

A short time after, Danielle asked me to accompany her on a delivery to homes on the outskirts of town where some of the elderly who could not come to the bakery lived. These walks soon became more frequent.

We usually would complete our deliveries in short time, strolling along garden paths and across meadows in early bloom. On the way back, we'd stopped at a hilly overlook and stretched out on a grassy area, staring at the sky and talking for hours. She was preparing for her *baccalauréat*, the final exam after the high school years. Although she was my age, her schooling was way ahead of mine, as I had to quit school at the age of fifteen to help my parents. We sang songs, recited poetry, told jokes and had a wonderful time.

Back working at the vineyard, I had the early morning shift. Most of my afternoons were free and we relished our time together. It was on a sunny June morning, while lying next to each other in the shade of a large elm tree, that she suddenly pulled me over and bringing her face close to mine, softly kissed me on my lips. I put my arms around her and, for a while, we just lay there whispering and caressing, enjoying that delightful nearness. Looking at me with eyes full of tenderness, Danielle slowly began shedding her clothes, taking the initiative with a joyful exuberance that would culminate in exhilarating bliss.

We must have dozed off, when a brief spring shower awoke us. Danielle turned to me and kissed my wet face.

"It was your first time, wasn't it?"

I frowned, then I nodded.

"Don't worry," she said, "it was wonderful."

For a brief moment we forgot the world around us, the war that was not going well, the daily vicissitudes of life and the uncertainty of what the future held in store for us.

As our relationship grew, I wanted to know more and more about her.

"Does it bother you that I am Jewish?" I asked her one day.

She burst out laughing, "Does it look like it?"

I had to laugh too, but the subject was never far from my mind. I inquired whether she was going to confession and she told me that she was.

"Are you telling him about us?" I wanted to know.

"Why do you ask?" she answered. "Let us just be happy and enjoy these days."

"Would you ever consider marrying me?" I kept on.

"Aren't you going to America after the war?"

"Yes, but you could come with me."

She smiled, shaking her head. "I don't think so. I am a French girl from the South and I plan to stay here." Then she added, snuggling up to me. "Ah, *mon cheri,* you will remember me though, won't you?"

The first week of July, she told me that she intended to leave Aubenas in the fall to enroll at the University of Lyon, to become a teacher for exceptional children. She seemed rather preoccupied and when I pushed her to tell me what was wrong, she finally told me that her brother had joined the "Maquis"—the local resistance group—and that she was terribly worried he might get killed.

She started to cry. "For God's sake, don't whisper a word to anybody!" she said, unable to stop sobbing.

"Of course not, Danielle. You know I won't," I assured her.

I hugged her and held her in my arms until she started to calm down.

Chapter Six

Family and Friends

Over the past few months we had received some urgent messages from my uncle Sigmund's family in Paris. Like us, he too had immigrated to Luxembourg in 1933. In 1938 he was offered a job in a small dental lab in Paris. A dentist by profession who had been unable to get a work permit in Luxembourg, he was only too happy to accept that position and a new start. That same year, my father had moved us to Brussels in the hope of finding work there, which would allow him to both reside and work in the same country.

My two cousins, Edgar and Leo, were like the brothers I never had. We practically lived in each other's house in Frankfurt and I missed them very much.

After the rapid defeat of France, my uncle's family found themselves trapped in the Occupied Zone under the direct control of the Germans. The messages were written by Edgar, who was fourteen at the time. In his first letter he mentioned that the French police had come for his father. He was only allowed to take just one small suitcase.

In the next card, sent a month later, Edgar informed us that he had heard from his father, who had been sent to Pithiviers, an internment camp near Paris, where he lived in barracks with fifty other inmates. He had assured them that he was okay, but did not give any other details. Apparently all mail was censored. Edgar added that his mother was taking in laundry from the neighbors to make ends meet and that little Leo was sick, coughing up blood.

In late May, he told us that his mother had to sell his stamp collection, his pride and joy, in order to buy food: "I still think it wasn't fair. Dad would be very unhappy if he knew. We started that collection when I was five years old." Later he wrote: "I have decided not to become a doctor like Dad. I am going to be a rabbi. Mom asked me why. I am not sure myself. Perhaps I can find the answer to why God is letting bad things happen to his people. We have very little food and are hungry all the time. Mom looks awful and I hear her cry at night. Our neighbor in the apartment below us has disappeared with his entire family."

The last message we received was dated June 10. It was from my aunt. She sounded very worried: "There are rumors that we will soon be sent to a labor camp in the east. Is it possible for Edgar and Leo to visit you?" We tried to make contacts to have the two children smuggled into the Unoccupied Zone, but then things started to unravel very rapidly.

We learned of massive roundups on July 16 and 17 in the Paris area. Thousands of foreign Jews, the majority of them women and children, had been herded into the Vélodrome d'Hiver, a former stadium for bicycle races. According to the British radio, most of them were sent to Pithiviers and Drancy, an unfinished apartment complex that was being used as a transit camp.

From there, the BBC reported, transports were going to the east, destination unknown. We were horrified by the news. Somehow my father, who had been an inveterate pessimist all these years, refused to believe that such a fate could be in store for us in Vichy France. He had hoped to survive these troubled times by living quietly, inconspicuously, in our small town, doing whatever the authorities asked of us, until the day France would be liberated. That day seemed very far off indeed.

German divisions stood at the gates of Stalingrad. Rommel's Africa Corps was pounding the defenses of El Alamein, the gateway to the Suez Canal, and America, a nation still reeling from the trauma of Pearl Harbor, was trying to come to grips with the realities of total war.

There was only one other Jewish family in Aubenas. Karl and Clara Flesch, a childless couple, had been our friends in Brussels. They too had left Germany in 1933 when the Nazis came to power.

In the first week of August, early one morning, there was a knock at our door. When we opened it, our friends stood there, obviously upset. My father motioned them in. Mr. Flesch was the first to speak. "We have some very disturbing news," he said. "Within the next ten days, all foreign Jews in the Unoccupied Zone will be rounded up and sent to the east." He paused a moment. "We were told that they would be shipped to work camps either in Germany or Poland. That is happening right now in Paris."

"How do you know this?" my father wanted to know.

"We have it from a very reliable source, one close to the prefect of the department."

"What can we do?" my father asked. "We can't run away. Everybody knows us here. Besides, I am sure every town exit is being watched. Even if we were able to get out, our identification papers with that big "J" on it would give us away."

"You are not just going to wait for them to arrest you and your family, are you?" Mr. Flesch asked, incredulous.

My father shrugged his shoulders. "What is the worst that can happen? That we will have to go to work for the Germans? I am sure they need manpower in their factories and on their farms with so many soldiers being sent to Russia. If our family can stay together, God willing, we will survive."

Mr. Flesch shook his head and raising his voice said, "You don't really think the Germans would treat the Jews like human beings, do you? The news from the Resistance is that there are special slave labor camps where people are being beaten and starved to death."

My father started to pace up and down. When he stopped, he turned toward my mother and me. "What do you think we ought to do?"

"We could hide in the country," I ventured.

My mother shook her head. "Who would hide us? Most farmers are antisemites who would just as well deliver us to the Germans."

Mr. Flesch stood up and put his hands on my father's shoulders. "Nathan, I have come here to tell you that I have found a way out." He hesitated a moment. "Clara and I have decided to convert to Catholicism."

My father took a step backwards. "You have done what?" he exclaimed.

"It is the only way, believe me. We have already made arrangements with the local priest to be baptized. He has contacted the diocese in Avignon. They are welcoming us with open arms and they promised to guarantee our safety. In fact, they have the assurance of the gendarmerie who is in charge of the roundups."

For a while my father just stood there, not saying anything. Finally, he spoke up. "I will not judge you, my friend. You must do what is best for you."

"There is something else," Mr. Flesch added. "I did not come here today only to give you the news. I have come to ask you to do the same."

"Oh, no!" my father cried out. "Never! We will not do that. We have gone through terrible times since 1933, but somehow God has watched over us. He won't abandon us. One day this terrible war will end, and God willing, we will survive. As Jews."

Clara Flesch turned to my mother. "Please Paula, talk to him. We are not taking this step because we do not love our faith. We are doing it because we are certain that we will not survive otherwise. Think of your son. What is the likelihood he will come through this alive?'

My father kept on shaking his head without uttering a word. Mr. Flesch raised his voice: "What about the Marranos during the Spanish Inquisition? They chose conversion just to escape execution. In their hearts they remained Jews. Were they wrong to do this to survive?"

"Perhaps not," my father answered with sadness in this voice, "but I cannot change who I am. Throughout the ages, Jews have been persecuted. There are very few instances where they abandoned their faith. Remember this part of the Twenty-third Psalm? 'Yea, though I walk through the valley of the shadow of death, I will fear no evil, for Thou art with me . . .'"

My father stopped and walked over to his friend. In a voice shaking with emotion, he said, "Please try to understand. To me the uniqueness of the Jewish people is the moral foundation of our belief. We have suffered through the ages, but we were never deterred from fulfilling those moral obligations. If I don't believe this, I have nothing to believe in."

Karl Flesch stood up slowly. His voice was resigned. There were tears in his eyes. "I am sorry I was unable to convince you, my friend, but I respect your beliefs. I only pray that, one day, we shall meet again."

Chapter Seven

The Escape

On the morning of August 20, as had been my daily routine, I was listening to the BBC bringing the latest news from London to occupied Europe. My parents were still asleep and I had the radio under my bed cover. I glanced at my mother in the next bed. She was tossing and turning in her sleep. She had worked until late into the night to finish two pairs of sandals she was supposed to deliver the next day. Her constant bouts with arthritis had made these tasks sheer agony.

The news report was at first garbled, until suddenly, the clipped voice of the announcer came through the airwaves, loud and clear: "This is a special announcement. In the early morning hours of August 19, expeditionary forces of the Seventh Canadian Division, supported by a flotilla of navy ships and the Royal Air Force, have crossed the English Channel and landed near the town of Dieppe on the northern coast of France."

I let out a scream that awoke both of my parents. "It's the Invasion!" I yelled, my voice choking with excitement. "They finally did it!"

"Keep your voice down!" my father admonished me. "Do you want everyone to hear you?"

I hoped to get additional information, but the voice on the radio had drifted off. Heavy jamming drowned out any messages. Within minutes, I was dressed and out the door.

"Where are you going?" my mother called after me.

"Down to the newspaper stand. Maybe the papers will have some more details."

A large and happy crowd, shouting and gesticulating, had picked up the few morning papers within minutes. The atmosphere seemed charged with a new found energy. Rumors were flying of additional Allied landings.

"It won't be long now," a young woman said, expressing what was on everyone's mind.

I had been lucky to get hold of one of the last papers. Clutching the special edition, I glanced at the headline: "Canadian Raid Repulsed with Heavy Losses to the Enemy!" I shrugged my shoulders. I really had not expected the German-controlled French press to announce anything else. I did not believe them.

How were we to know that this was indeed just a commando raid and that the real invasion would not take place until two years later? I rolled up the paper, waving it like a banner. Running at full speed to give my parents the news, I soon turned onto our street and froze in my tracks. Less than a hundred feet away in front of our house, an open truck stood packed with men. In spite of the summer heat, they all wore hats and overcoats.

My mouth went dry and my heart started to pound wildly. I spotted my father, carrying a small suitcase as he walked toward the truck with two gendarmes towering over him. My mother, screaming frantically, was held back by the two sisters with whom we were staying. The gendarmes motioned him to climb into the truck. When he could not swing himself up, they simply lifted his frail, worn-out body and deposited him next to the others. He too wore a coat but no hat.

The realization of what was happening in front of my eyes hit me like lightning. For weeks we had heard rumors of massive roundups in the north and deportations to the east. Somehow, because of our work status in the Unoccupied Zone, we had hoped to escape that fate. Now they had come for us!

One of the gendarmes looked in my direction. Our eyes met for an instant. Slowly, deliberately, he began to climb off the truck. I turned on my heels and started to race through the cobblestone streets. The sound of boots hitting the pavement seemed to come closer and closer. Glancing back I caught a glimpse of a black uniform. Panic doubled my strength. I crisscrossed the town, in and out of alleys, along garden patches and over fences. I was running for my life. A sharp pain in my side forced me to stop. The street seemed quiet. The gendarme had apparently given up his pursuit.

I found myself in front of a tobacco store where only days before I had bought cigarettes for my father. When I walked through the door, the proprietor, a short, balding man greeted me with a smile. Still grasping for breath and barely able to speak, I told him what had happened.

"Please hide me," I begged. "I have no place to go."

His eyes narrowed and his face froze; he raised his hands as if in despair.

"I am sorry," he whispered, "but I cannot hide you." He pointed to a sign on his counter that identified him as a member of Pétain's Legionnaires, the despised standard bearers of the new order and collaborators with the Germans.

"I am sorry," he kept on repeating, "but you understand, don't you?" With that he pushed me out of the door and locked it after me. For a moment I just stood there, unable to move. Desperate and gripped with fear, I started to run until I reached the town limit.

Hidden partially behind a giant chestnut tree was a small but well kept cottage. It belonged to an eighty-six-year-old widow and former schoolteacher. Now nearly blind, she lived there with her sixty-year-old daughter. I had occasionally run errands for them. With trembling hands I rang the bell. The daughter opened the door, and seeing how exhausted I was, motioned me inside. Her mother was sitting in a rocking chair. After I told them what had happened, the old woman lifted herself out of her chair. She stood erect, turned her unseeing eyes in my direction and opened her arms wide.

Pressing me close to her chest, she said in a soft voice, "I am sorry to have lived this long only to witness this day of shame for France. You will stay here with us, my son. You will be safe here, I promise you." Then she hugged me and wept.

After I had rested a while, I was able to organize my thoughts. I told them that I could not stay. I had to find out where they had taken my father and what happened to my mother. "Perhaps I could slip out later, under the cover of darkness," I suggested.

The two women were aghast. "You will stay here and not endanger yourself." The old woman's voice was firm. "I will send my daughter to your place. She knows the two widows. Without of course breathing a word about you, she will find out what you want to know and your mind will be at ease." She then led me to a sofa in the living room and told me to rest.

I closed my eyes, but was unable to sleep. I kept retracing in my mind our long odyssey. From the early days in Frankfurt through the start of the war, the Polish Army, the camp and the work I had to perform at the vineyard. In spite of all the hardships, we had hoped to wait out the war in this small town. And now it had all come to an end. Fate had caught up with us.

It must also have been Fate that made me rush to the kiosk for the newspaper in those early morning hours. If not for that announcement by the BBC, I too would have been on that truck.

An hour passed and the daughter returned. She had been unable to talk to my mother directly, who, according to the sisters, was near a breakdown. She had begged the gendarmes to take her too, so that she could be with her husband and her son. One of the gendarmes had taken her aside and told her that her turn would come in two days. His instructions at this point were to arrest the men only. "Your son better be here when we come back," he added ominously.

My mind was made up now. I had to be with her. My friends tried to dissuade me, but when they saw that I was determined, they embraced me. "May God watch over you," they said with tears in their eyes.

When I walked through our door, my mother looked at me as if she saw a ghost. She had feared that I too had been captured. She touched my face and hands over and over again, sobbing uncontrollably. There was a knock at the door. Giselle, the older sister walked in holding a cup of tea in her hand. She seemed surprised to see me. "How come you are here?" she asked. Her eyes seemed strangely cold. "Where were you when they came for your father?" I did not answer her.

Turning toward my mother, she said, "I found out where they have taken your husband. According to the driver, the men were taken to Fort Barreaux, a prison nearby, awaiting their transport to Drancy near Paris. There was talk of families being resettled in labor camps in Germany. "That's not too bad," she added. "Many of our French boys are working for the Germans right now."

After Giselle had left, we debated our options all through the night. We were trapped in a town where everybody knew us. There was no doubt that the bus and train stations were being watched. It looked hopeless. By morning we decided to join my father at the detention center. My mother packed a small suitcase and I went out to buy some provisions and a first aid kit. I was about to enter the pharmacy when I felt a hand on my shoulder. It was Danielle and she was visibly upset.

"What in the world are you doing here?" she exclaimed, grabbing my arm. "Don't you know what's going on?"

I nodded and told her about my father's arrest and our decision to join him.

"Are you out of your mind?" she asked. My brother has information from the Resistance. Trains filled with men, women and children are leaving day and night from Paris in the direction of Poland. The Germans have erected giant concentration camps, not work camps. The conditions are indescribable. People are being used for slave labor. Many have died from hunger, illness and beatings!"

"But how are we to get out of here?" I asked. "We have only our refugee cards."

She hesitated a moment, "I will tell you how. Go home. Take a few belongings, just a small bag. In fifteen minutes my father and I will be in front of your place. When you see us, put the satchel down. I will pick it up. You both stroll behind us. My father will purchase two tickets to the next stop and put the valise on the train. When the train is about to pull out, you jump on it. The next station is Valence. From there trains are leaving every few hours for Grenoble, near the border, where I'm sure you will find help to crossover." Then she embraced me and whispered "God be with you, *mon amour*."

Everything went as she had planned. My courageous Danielle had shown us the way. The train was packed with people. It was Friday, market day in Valence. After a while, I got up from my cramped quarters and moved slowly from compartment to compartment. Suddenly, I came to a halt. A group of youngsters between the ages of seven and ten, dressed in blue and yellow scout uniforms, were singing, led by a tiny woman, the apparent leader of the troop. I took a seat next to her. She gave me a friendly smile. Hesitating only a moment, I whispered, "I must talk to you."

Her smile faded and her eyes narrowed as she stared at me. However, she listened intently without interrupting as I told her my story. Somehow I felt that I could confide in her. When I finished, she took my hand. "Bring your mother here. You will both stay with us until Valence, when we will all get off the train. Keep yourself busy with the children. You are now part of our group. Just leave the talking to me."

In Valence, the woman led the procession. We followed, gently nudging the slower children. At the gate, two gendarmes stood immobile watching the crowd. With barely a glance, they let the noisy gang and their guardians walk through. Outside the station, the woman scribbled a name and address on a piece of paper.

"Go see this young man," she said. "He is Dutch and a friend of mine. Tell him Nicole sent you. He may be able to help you. Good luck." She grasped my hand and she and her flock were gone. The name on the paper was Pieter Hooft. He lived at 33 rue Anatole France.

The streets were jammed with bicycles, horse drawn carts and a few isolated trucks. Women were lining up in front of grocery stores waiting for the weekly arrival of fruits and vegetables brought in by farmers to supplement their meager monthly rations.

I noticed a gendarme standing at the street corner and walked over to him. He gave me a probing glance. "Could you tell me how to get to rue Anatole France?" I asked. He pointed to his left. "See that street behind the park? That's it. You are practically there."

Number 33 turned out to be a narrow two-story building badly in need of repair. I rang the bell and a woman's gruff voice answered: "What do you want?" I had forgotten about that timeless character of French culture, the concierge, who must screen every visitor before granting permission to enter the premises.

"I would like to see Pieter Hooft," I said. "I am a friend of his aunt Nicole."

I heard the buzzer. Motioning my mother to wait outside, I pushed the door open. The small hallway was in semi-darkness. I was barely able to see the stairs leading to the upper floor. The door from where that voice had come was slightly ajar. I caught a glimpse of an elderly woman of enormous proportions squatting on an overstuffed chair like some giant bug, her hair in rollers, a pair of glasses on the very tip of her nose, looking through a magazine.

"What's your name?" she hissed without getting up.

"Jean . . . Jean Chaulet." I could only think of the name of the old lady and her daughter who had given me shelter that fateful morning.

The woman lifted herself up with what seemed a superhuman effort and turning toward the stairs, yelled at the top of her lungs: "Pieter, someone to see you!" Moments later, a tall young man with a shock of blond wavy hair came sauntering down the stairs.

"I have greetings from your aunt Nicole," I said.

Hesitating for just a moment, the young man broke out in a big smile. "Of course, and how is my dear aunt?"

"She is fine." I sensed the concierge's eyes upon me.

"Come on up," Pieter told me.

I shook my head. "I am actually in quite a hurry. Why don't you walk me back to the station and I'll tell you all about her." Pieter nodded and we walked out into the street where my mother had been waiting nervously.

"This is my mother," I said. "I didn't want her to come in. Her French is not the best."

"I am a burden to my son," my mother said, smiling sadly.

"Pay no attention to her," I laughed, "she just wants your sympathy."

Pieter pointed to the nearby park with a number of empty benches. "Let's sit here," he suggested. "We won't be disturbed."

Once more, I told my story, including the chance encounter with Nicole. When I had finished, Pieter kept quiet for a few moments.

"The most urgent thing is to provide you with forged French papers. Without them you won't be able to go far. I will try to contact the man who does that work. In the meantime, you will stay with me and my roommate. His name is Andre and he is a medical student. Next, we have to get you both into our room without Madame Legrand, the concierge, being aware of it." He smiled at our perplexed look.

"I will brief Andre and then go down to wait at the front door. Andre will join me in a few minutes. We will keep the door slightly ajar while we engage the lady in conversation. She loves to chatter. I will give you a signal by putting my hand on my head. You then will both slip behind our backs up the stairs and into our place. The door will be open."

It worked perfectly. The room was dimly lit. Two unmade beds, a table loaded with books and clothes piled just everywhere, greeted us. Pieter moved a small dresser revealing a trap door about two feet high and two feet wide. He slid through it and motioned us to follow him. Narrow winding stairs led to a small attic with a very low ceiling making it impossible to stand up. A ray of light came through a tiny porthole.

Here we lived for the next two weeks. Once a day, our protectors brought us water and food. At night we spent some time in their room to regain circulation in our legs and clean up. Because we never knew when Madame Legrand might suddenly check on the boys, we hardly left our hiding place, except to use the toilet, which was located in back of the house. The two kept watch until we were back safely.

We learned that both young men had fled Holland when the Germans invaded their country in 1940 and had been living in Valence for the past two years.

One evening we heard a knock at their door. We were unable to understand the muffled voices. After a while, Pieter gave us a signal and I slipped down the stairs. "It was the police," he said. "They were just checking our papers. They found them in order and there was no problem. However, we cannot take the risk of a repeat visit, one that might lead to your detection. I am going to check on that forger. He's been swamped with work, but I'll tell him that this is an emergency."

At the end of the week, Pieter came back with two French identification cards. My name was now Charles Fontaine from St. Omer, a small town near Calais on the northern coast of France. My mother's name was Nadine. The cards were crudely made. The forger had taken out our old photos and pasted them on the new cards. He had circled the part of the official stamp that was missing on the new card with a black crayon. According to Pieter, the regular man had been arrested two days earlier and his replacement was not too good. "Let's hope nobody will look that closely," he said. He then produced a map of the area and pointed to Grenoble. "That's your best bet to cross into Switzerland," he told us.

We left the next day, thanking our friends for all their help. We had offered to pay for the new papers, but they refused. "We have a contingency fund," he added. I suspected that they both were active in the Resistance, but I refrained from probing and they never brought up the subject.

We caught the train for Grenoble just in time. It was late in the afternoon when we arrived. The sunset casting a pink hue over majestic Mont Blanc was spectacular.

We walked through the city's wide streets lined with trees in full bloom in search of the synagogue, where we hoped to get help and shelter. When we finally got there, we found the doors locked and no one in sight. For a while, we just walked aimlessly through the streets. Darkness had come rather suddenly and we became increasingly alarmed at the prospect of being unable to find a place for the night when we came upon a large building, apparently a hotel.

Lights were visible behind partially drawn curtains, defying strict orders of the blackout. Incredibly, strains of music, rarely heard since France's defeat, reached our ears. Hungry and tired, we decided to check out the place. The brightly lit hotel lobby was packed with people. At the reception desk, an elderly woman was busy filing index cards. When we approached her, she looked up and greeted us.

I told her that we needed a room for the night. She looked at us pensively. Lowering her voice, she whispered, "Are you Jewish?"

I shook my head in denial. My mother, at the same time, said, "Yes, we are."

The woman nodded. There was sadness in her voice. " I know what is happening to you poor people." She glanced around furtively. "I'm going to give you a room for the night. I must write your name on my register cards. If they check on me, I have to protect myself. However I will 'misplace' that card in a different file."

She hesitated a moment before going on. "You see, this hotel serves as the headquarters for the German occupation forces in Grenoble."

My mother grabbed my hand. "Don't worry," the woman went on, "tomorrow morning at six o'clock I will tap three times at your door so you will know it is me. I shall bring you to the station myself where you will catch the 6:45 train for Annemasse, the nearest border town, just across from Geneva." Then she led us to a small room on the top floor.

We barely closed our eyes all night. Early in the morning, as promised, the woman knocked at our door using the prearranged signal. We followed her down the stairs and into the street, passing some German soldiers who greeted us courteously.

At the station she bought two tickets for us and refused to be reimbursed. She embraced us with tears in her eyes, saying "When you arrive safely in Switzerland, please send me a post card with just the word 'Greetings.' I will know it is from you." The train departed five minutes later.

After traveling for half an hour, my mother became increasingly restless. "Let's get off at the next stop," she urged. "I have a strange feeling about this train." Although I objected to this change of plans, I finally agreed. Much later, we found out that this train had been thoroughly searched at Annemasse and many people had been arrested. Her premonition had saved us.

By a stroke of luck, the place where we got off the train had a bus connection to Taninges, another town near the border. The bus was packed despite the early hour. Soon we were traveling on a narrow mountain road. I studied the faces of the passengers. Three men and a woman caught my eye. They were talking in whispers. All of them carried heavy rucksacks with wool covers rolled around them.

On the spur of the moment, I began to whistle a French folk tune, changing abruptly to the first few bars of "Hatikvah," the Jewish national anthem. The older man in the group glanced in my direction. After a few moments he began to whistle. My mother and I looked at each other. He had just finished the second stanza of "Hatikvah."

At the third bus stop, the four got off. Swiftly we followed them. "What do you want?" the older man wanted to know. He did not sound too friendly.

"Obviously we are all in the same boat," I replied. "We too intend to go over the mountains. We would like to join you."

The young man in the group, apparently the guide, spoke up. "No way!" he said emphatically. "We must go over dangerous mountain passes for ten hours or more. Your mother would never make it."

No amount of pleading would change their minds. We offered what little money we had left, but they stood firm in their determination not to let us accompany them. In despair, we watched them disappear. We were stranded in this tiny hamlet, just miles away from the border. After our initial shock, we noticed a small inn at the foot of the mountain road. Since there was no bus until the next morning, we decided to stay there overnight. The man behind the desk handed us the registration forms.

"I see you are from St. Omer," he beamed. "That is my home town."

Oh no, I thought.

"I haven't been back in ten years," he added, much to my relief.

A good night's sleep refreshed us both. Early in the morning, we started the ascent on our own, without a guide, without maps, and without the slightest idea what sort of terrain lay ahead. After two hours of walking on a gradually increasing incline, the grade became much steeper. We were both worn out and had to sit down. Suddenly there was some rustling in the bushes. We were startled to see two men appear holding a woman who was crying as if in agony. Her hair was disheveled. She wore no shoes and her feet were swollen and bloody. The men did not look much better. All three seemed near exhaustion. We recognized the group who had left us stranded the day before.

Haltingly they told us that after hours of steep climbing, they had taken a nap. When they woke up the young guide had disappeared with all their money. They had walked for hours through snow-covered terrain until by accident they had found a road leading back to their starting point.

"Your mother would never have made it," the older man told me. "If you continue in that direction," he added, pointing ahead, "you will run straight into the arms of the border guard." Then they left us.

For a while, we just stood there. We had come so close. With nobody to help us over the mountains and our ration cards about to expire, we decided to return to the interior of the country. Lyon, some hundred miles to the west, seemed the place to regroup and plan for another attempt. Our hearts were heavy. "There will be another day," I promised, comforting my mother.

We arrived in France's second largest city in the afternoon and immediately contacted the Jewish relief committee. At that time, French Jews had not been included in the deportations. Their time would come a few months later.

We were given the address of a Jewish doctor from Tunisia who had been hiding more than fifty men, women and children in his large home. Here we received food and shelter for the next ten days. There was only one rule. Everybody had to be out of the house during the day. We could only return at nightfall so as not to raise the suspicions of the neighbors.

All throughout the day, police vans, their sirens blasting, combed the city, closing off entire blocks. Anyone whose papers were not in order and who was unfortunate enough to get caught in their net was arrested. We spent eight to ten hours in movie houses, where for a while we hoped to escape the constant danger. Each night fewer and fewer people returned to the shelter.

It had been seven weeks since that fateful morning in August when my father was arrested. The first chill of October had descended over the region. Before the weather made escape impossible, we decided to try again. I studied the map of the border area with renewed intensity, slowly devising a plan that I felt was foolproof.

I picked a village, some five miles from the border, called La Chapelle d'Abondance. I was sure that there would be a chapel and a priest. As a man of God, he would come to our aid.

I wrote a letter addressed to myself, presumably coming from a cousin who invited us to his baby's baptism in Abondance. Should I be questioned so close to the border, I would have this ready-made excuse.

My mother and I were both blond and we did not look Jewish. I wore the traditional French beret and carried a copy of the *Gringoire,* a newspaper known for its pro-German editorials. My mother wore a large cross around her neck. Indeed, we did give a very good imitation of ardent collaborators of the new order.

The first step was to take the train to Annecy, where many bus connections to the border originated. The scheduled train showed a stop at Aix-les-Bains, the famous spa. All went as planned. We arrived at Aix on time. The train was to pull out ten minutes later. At the end of thirty minutes, an announcement was made. Because of engine trouble, the train would not go on. There would be another train at ten o'clock that evening. We were stunned. This meant that we would be unable to connect with that bus to Abondance. To stay even one more day in this region was fraught with danger and unthinkable.

The large square outside the station was nearly empty. We sat down on a bench under a chestnut tree, despair in our hearts. We felt this was the end of the line for us. "Maybe it was not meant to be," my mother said, her voice breaking.

Across the square, about a hundred feet away, a long, gray limousine had pulled up. From its right fender flapped a small flag with a swastika on it. We looked at each other. My mother pressed my hand slightly.

"Make sure not to say word," I cautioned her. Her French was still laced with a heavy German accent. "Put a scarf around your neck. You have a severe case of laryngitis if anyone should ask."

Briskly I walked up to the car. An officer of the Wehrmacht, studying a large map, looked up. "Pardon me, sir," I said, "our train developed engine trouble. We have to attend a baptism and must catch the bus for Abondance. Could you give us a lift?" My heart pounded in my ears.

He hesitated a moment. In good, though accented French, he explained that his destination was Annecy. If that would help us, we were welcome.

I thanked him and helped my mother into the back seat. "I am waiting for another person to join us," he told me.

"Is there time for me to buy some fruit at the grocery store?" I inquired. "We have not eaten all day." He agreed that indeed, there was time.

When I returned with my bag of apples, the car was nowhere in sight. I panicked. Cursing my stupidity, I ran across the square. Just then, the car emerged from a side street. A civilian was sitting next to the officer. I prayed silently that my mother had kept her mouth shut. Spotting me, she stuck her head out of the car window and yelled "HELLO!" at the top of her lungs, pronouncing the "H" as no Frenchman was capable of doing. The officer and his companion, engaged in conversation, paid no attention to this nearly fatal slip. I climbed into the back seat.

The newcomer, who wore a black leather overcoat, seemed to be in command. After discussing a few details concerning the trip, he wanted to know when the German army had begun giving civilians a lift. He sounded annoyed. The officer repeated my story word for word.

"I hope the Wehrmacht is not helping Jews to escape." His laugh had a sardonic ring to it. My mother tensed beside me and I froze where I sat. We didn't dare to look at each other. Through the rear view mirror, we saw his eyes focused on us. I grabbed an apple and took a healthy bite out of it. I believe what saved us was the fact that he did not for moment consider it a serious possibility.

The car rushed through small villages at great speed. We passed French militia on their motorcycles waiting at cross points. They were stopping all cars, that is, except the car with the swastika.

Meanwhile the officer engaged me in conversation. He unleashed a tirade against the French, whom he called lazy and soft, and who should do their share for the new order of Europe. I agreed. His next topic was the war. Much to my surprise he explained that Germany did not expect to defeat the Americans.

"Once we are through with the Russians, we will have a peace of compromise," he told me.

I dared to question him with the nerve of a youth. "Why have you not taken Leningrad as yet?" He exclaimed that two million dead Russians were causing cholera around that city and that it was just as easy to starve the inhabitants to death.

"What about the Jews?" I asked, tempting fate.

"What about them?" he replied curtly. He seemed irritated.

"Aren't they being deported from France?"

"Lies, nothing but lies," he exclaimed loudly. I did not go so far as proving him wrong.

"By the way," he wanted to know, "do you speak German?"

"Unfortunately, no," I replied. "Next year we will study it."

Within an hour we had reached Annecy. The officer, bowing courteously, bid us farewell. He regretted that he was unable to be of further service to us. I assured him that he had been of invaluable help and he seemed pleased.

The civilian did not give us a second look. As we got out of the car a few French women standing on the sidewalk stared at us with contempt. We had made excellent time, but still had to reach the bus depot which was near the train station about two miles from where the car had let us off. Flagging down a taxi, I told the driver that we had to catch the bus for Abondance to get us to a baptism on time.

"No problem," he said. "Just a point of information. Down the road the gendarmes are stopping all cars. Seems they are looking for Jews trying to escape over the mountains into Switzerland."

"What has that got to do with us?" I managed to put some indignation into my voice.

He shrugged his shoulders and opened the door. We had driven less than three hundred feet when we were stopped by a gendarme. He looked into the car and politely asked us for our identification cards. He studied them at great length without uttering a word. His eyes darted from me to my mother and back to me again.

My heart was racing. Perspiration was trickling down my neck. After what seemed an eternity, he handed the papers back and motioned us to move on. When I glanced through the rear window, I saw him tip his hat slightly.

The cab brought us to the bus on time. We reached Abondance in the evening. We found the priest, a kindly, white haired man in his seventies to whom we told our plan to escape to freedom. Without hesitating, he offered us food and shelter. "Have a good night's rest," he told us. "You will need all your strength for tomorrow."

Chapter Eight

Arrival in Switzerland

The next morning, shortly after six, the priest knocked at our door. We were already dressed and ready. Pointing to his maid who had come into the room with him, he said, "This is Ginette. She will guide you to the border. Just follow her. She knows every inch of that mountain. You will be safe." Then he hugged us and said "God bless you both."

Ginette was a short, plump woman in her forties wearing a black skirt and a black sweater. Her hair was covered with a gray wool cap. She carried a small backpack. "I have some provisions in here," she said with a bright smile, "bread, cheese and water. I will be about fifty feet ahead of you. If you get tired, whistle and we will take a rest. Only whisper to each other; I don't expect any problems, but we must be careful. If I do encounter anything suspicious, I'll stop and give you a signal, like this." With that she raised her arms and clasped her hands as if in prayer.

After two hours on the road, which was gradually getting steeper, Ginette stopped and motioned us to sit down. "We are now getting into the dense underbrush and the climbing will become harder. I'll make sure you are following me."

The ground was damp and muddy. Some patches were covered with a thin layer of early October snow. We used our hands to grasp branches that blocked our view while trying to keep our balance. Suddenly, my mother lost her footing and tumbled backwards. I rushed to her and helped her up. She was bleeding from a rather large cut on her left arm caused by the razor sharp twigs. I made a provisional bandage with my handkerchief. After she assured me that she was fine, we moved on.

Holding on tightly to her right hand, I continued pushing forward, clearing the bushes in front of me with my other hand. Ginette kept on climbing without stopping or hesitating. At times it seemed to us that she was going in circles, but soon we moved closer and closer to the tree line looming above us, which we knew would be our crossing point.

After two more hours of walking, with just a few minutes of rest, I motioned Ginette to take a break. I could see how exhausted my mother was. She had always suffered from arthritis and was obviously in great pain. We sat down and Ginette handed us some food and water.

We resumed our climb for another twenty minutes when Ginette abruptly raised her arms and clasped her hands. We slumped to the ground and remained motionless. After what seemed an eternity, Ginette came back to us. "Everything is fine. I saw something moving, but it was only a deer."

Thirty minutes later, she stopped. Turning around she waved us on, and when we reached her, she pointed to the east. "There is Switzerland. Be careful going down. God be with you." Then she embraced us and walked into the woods.

We had arrived at a clearing, seemingly the crest of a mountain pass. The trees had become sparse and a sudden burst of cold air made us shiver in spite of our jackets. At that elevation they provided little protection.

We had hoped the descent would be easier than the climb, but were sadly mistaken. I had to hold on to my mother with all my strength to prevent her from falling as we stumbled over twigs, tree stumps and loose stones, while trying to grab protruding branches to slow our descent on that slippery slope.

We were near exhaustion when we saw a figure some hundred feet below. A uniformed man was looking at us through binoculars. He proceeded to climb in our direction and reached us within minutes. The young, clean-shaven soldier looked at me with a stern face. His manner was curt and unfriendly.

"What year were you born?" he asked. He did not welcome us, nor did he show the slightest concern though it was obvious that my mother was in great distress. All he wanted to know was in what year I was born. Not my age, just the year.

Fortunately I was prepared for such a reception. At our hideout at the doctor's residence in Lyon, I had met a young man who had told me of his experience. After reaching the Swiss border he was confronted by a guard who asked him for his year of birth. He told him the correct date, he had just turned twenty, and was promptly escorted back to the French side.

It seemed the Germans had put pressure on the Swiss to refuse entry to all men between the ages of eighteen and forty-five, whom they feared might wind up fighting on the side of the Allies. While this young man managed to find his way back into the interior, most of the 30,000 refugees sent back by the Swiss authorities would fall into the hands of the Germans. Only a handful survived the war.

"I was born on May 10, 1925," I told him, making myself two years younger in the process. I had turned nineteen four months earlier. My mother had been leaning against a tree a few feet behind me and I was not sure whether she had heard me, so I repeated my answer for her benefit. "I was born in May 10, 1925, and my mother was born on April 18, 1898," I added, though he had not asked for her date of birth. My mother nodded imperceptibly.

Without uttering another word, and without offering any assistance, he motioned us to follow him. The descent took another two hours.

It was close to six o'clock in the evening when we arrived, completely exhausted, at a military post on the outskirts of a town called Champery. Our guard led us to a large tent, where a hundred men and women and a few children were waiting to be processed. Most of them had small bundles and all apparently had crossed the border at some point in their flight from France. A tall blond officer behind a makeshift desk was carefully examining the papers the refugees were handing him.

In the fall of 1942, Switzerland was an anomaly. Surrounded on all sides by the Axis powers in control of Continental Europe, it was like an island untouched by the inferno at its borders. Food, though rationed, was plentiful. There was full employment and commerce with both warring parties continued. Borders seemed secure as it apparently was in the interest of the nations at war to have that small country in the center of Europe maintain its neutral status.

When the deportations started in the summer of that year, that neutrality was seriously put to a test. While adhering to a longstanding policy of giving asylum to those trying to flee from persecution and in danger for their lives, there was also the reality that challenging the perpetrators could be tantamount to national suicide.

Switzerland decided on a middle course, accepting some 30,000 mostly Jewish refugees whose only hope was that magic island of peace, while at the same time under pressure by the Germans, pursuing a policy of turning down an equal number of men between the ages of eighteen and forty-five. We had crossed the border when that policy was in full force. Miraculously we had survived that near fatal encounter with the border guard. As we were standing in line waiting to be processed, our hearts were gripped with fear of what was in store for us.

We decided not to present our fake French papers. Instead, we filled out the forms handed to us, giving both our true names and dates of birth. To our immense relief, the officer gave them a scant glance. He wrote our names in a ledger and motioned us on.

We had escaped to freedom.

Two women in Red Cross uniforms began handing out baskets of fruit and bottles of water. An army nurse was checking medicine bottles she had lined up on a folding table. By now, my mother was having excruciating back pains and her hands needed bandaging.

I called the nurse over, who promptly made my mother lie down on one of the army cots at the rear of the tent. She took her vitals, put bandages on her hands and gave her medicine for her pain. "You will shortly be transported to the refugee camp at Bex, a town close by, where you will get the proper care," she said in a reassuring voice. When the processing was completed, we were directed to the front of the tent, where two army trucks stood waiting to take us to Bex.

The ride took less than twenty minutes. The driver told us that we were to be housed in a former school building that had been fixed up to provide temporary shelter. The smell of fresh paint greeted us as we walked through the doors. The classrooms had been converted into living quarters with six beds in each room, a table, two chairs and a large cardboard closet. Community showers were at the end of the hallway. Everything was clean and well scrubbed.

An officer, who had come into the room, explained that this facility was for women and children only, and that after supper, the men would be brought to another reception center in the town of Aigle an hour away.

My mother had been given a bed near the window. The medicine seemed to have done its job. "I feel so much better," she said, pressing my hand.

Ringing a hand-held bell to get our attention, a soldier announced that dinner was being served. The rows of wooden benches were rapidly filled by the famished crowd. Two women lugging enormous milk cans swiftly moved from table to table, heaping their contents—polenta, a porridge of mashed corn and applesauce—onto tin plates. We were told that this was a Swiss specialty called "heaven and earth." The mixture was delicious and filling. It looked like a good beginning.

After the meal the men said goodbye to their wives and children and boarded the bus for Aigle. I promised my mother I would contact her in the morning and assured her that everything was going to be fine.

It was close to ten o'clock when we arrived at a military compound where two barracks had been set aside for us, each lined with a hundred army cots. I was dead tired and could not wait to crash for the night.

In the morning two soldiers led us to a woodsy area, partially under water. We were handed shovels and picks and told to dig a trench forty feet long and ten feet wide for the purpose of laying an underground electrical cable.

A dour looking corporal sitting on a tree stump was watching us with indifference. After four hours, we took a fifteen-minute break and received some bread and apple cider. At six o'clock the corporal marched us back to the barracks.

I was worn out and all the bones in my body ached from the hard physical labor that I was not used to, but I felt this was a small price to pay for our freedom. I was grateful to the Swiss for having given us asylum and believed I should work for my keep.

I had not been able to contact my mother and was anxious to get a pass to visit her. The officer in charge, a young lieutenant, told me that I would soon be able to see her. "We have a good number of you people coming over the border every day. It does take some time to get things organized. Just be patient."

A few days later, a young woman from the Jewish committee in Geneva arrived. She interviewed our group, taking notes, and inquired if anybody had family in the United States or Canada; she offered to contact them. She also handed out some pocket money so that we could purchase a few items at the canteen and told us that a small allowance would be given to us within the next few days. Finally she made a list of heavy clothing we would need with the colder weather coming and promised to have them delivered very shortly. A guard had given me a post card and I asked her whether she would mail it for me.

"I have no stamp," I said, "but I promised someone very special in Grenoble to let her know of my arrival in Switzerland." She assured me that she would mail it the same day. The card had only one word on it: *"Salutations"* (Greetings). That wonderful lady at the hotel desk in Grenoble, our savior, would know who sent the message. And she would be happy.

Our work routine continued over the next few days. I was given the job, together with another young fellow from Luxembourg, Marcel Stern, to push a wheelbarrow around the perimeter where six men were digging, shoveling and piling up mountains of stones and gravel. Marcel and I would fill the wheelbarrow and roll it to a designated spot, empty its contents and go back for more. We had no idea where all those loads would wind up.

The next day my name was called while I was having my evening meal. A soldier led me to a room behind the mess hall. An officer was sitting behind a small desk. When I entered the place, he looked up.

"Are you the son of Paula Rubinstein?" he wanted to know.

I nodded. My heart started to pound. He hesitated a moment.

"Your mother suffered a mild heart attack," he said.

I put my hand to my mouth. "Oh no!" I managed to say.

"She is all right and under good care. It seems one of the women in her barrack had told her that you had been sent back over the border. She said that she had gotten the information from a reliable source."

"A heart attack!" I exclaimed. "I must see her at once! Please take me to her!"

"You will see her in the morning. She has been brought to the hospital in Bex where she is now resting comfortably."

All through the night, I was pacing the grounds in front of our compound, waiting for daybreak. Finally, around seven in the morning, two soldiers came for me. We got into a waiting car and reached the hospital in short time.

A nurse led me to a large white unadorned room with ten beds aligned against the wall. My mother's bed was at the end of the row. She had tubes in her nostrils and an IV in her arm. When she saw me, she tried to sit up, but slumped back on her pillow. I walked over to her and embraced her. She kept on hugging and touching me and did not want to let go.

"You see," I said, "I am here and I am fine. Do not worry any more. Nothing will happen to us. We are safe. Just get well." The head nurse told me that my mother would be released in a few days, provided there were no further complications.

We spent some time together, just holding hands. I promised to come back shortly. I was furious at the woman for having put my mother's life in jeopardy by circulating that rumor. For a moment I considered confronting her, but in the end I decided that there was no point in it.

It was only on the way back that the realization started to sink in, how close I had come to losing my mother—after all we had gone through.

*The synagogue that we attended in Frankfurt am Main, ca. 1932. It was burnt down dur-
ing Kristallnacht, November 9, 1938, and never rebuilt.*

With three friends in Revel, a town in the south of France, in 1940. Five days later, I was drafted into the Polish army.

My father wrote this letter to the Commandant of the camp at Agde on behalf of the 1,200 interned men, women and children. His efforts resulted in receiving a great number of food and clothing parcels.

In Aubenas, we rented a room in the house of two sisters, Genevieve and Giselle Martin, shown here with their mother on their balcony.

With Danielle, the baker's daughter, in the spring of 1942. Danielle helped us flee Aubenas during the roundups.

The Klausner family: My uncle Sigmund, his wife Lola, and their sons Edgar, 6, and Leo, 2. Like us, they had fled Frankfurt for Luxembourg in 1933.

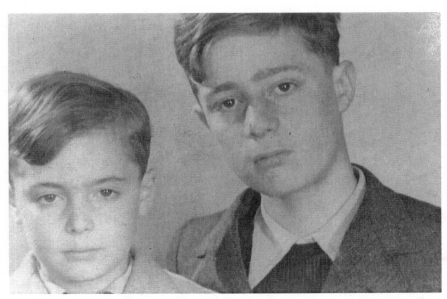

My cousins Edgar, 14, and Leo, 10, in Paris. In September 1942, they were deported to the concentration camp at Auschwitz where they died.

My parents with their friends, Karl and Clara Flesch. My father is in the middle, my mother at the far right.

Our last outing in Aubenas, four days before my father's arrest on August 20, 1942.

Fort Barreaux, the prison where my father was taken after his arrest. From there, he was sent to the French transit camp at Drancy.

Revisiting France thirty-four years later, I am standing in front of the kiosk where I got the newspaper announcing the Allied landing in Dieppe on the northern coast of France. It was also the day that the roundups began in Unoccupied France.

I remember these streets where I ran for my life, with the gendarme in hot pursuit.

In Aix-les-Bains, my mother and I hitched a ride with a German officer to reach a border town for our escape.

The church in La Chapelle d'Abondance, where the priest helped us and his maid Ginette led us across the Alps to Switzerland.

At the Swiss work camp Bonstetten: I am on the left, my friend Walter Sperling is on the right.

At the Children's Home at Speicher: I am skiing with Walter, the young violinist.

Playing chess with my students Pierre, Maurice, Henri, Marcel, and Camille. This photo was in our student newspaper.

COMITÉ INTERNATIONAL DE LA CROIX-ROUGE

SERVICE INTERNATIONAL DE RECHERCHES

3548 Arolsen · République fédérale d'Allemagne

INTERNATIONAL TRACING SERVICE

3548 Arolsen · Federal Republic of Germany

INTERNATIONALER SUCHDIENST

3548 Arolsen · Bundesrepublik Deutschland

Telephone: Arolsen 434 · Télégrammes: ITS Arolsen

SM/JB/ej

Sehr geehrter Herr Rubinstein!

Wir beziehen uns auf Ihre obenangeführte Suchanfrage und teilen Ihnen
mit, daß beim Internationalen Suchdienst über die unter Betreff aufge-
führten Personen folgende Angaben vorliegen:

1) RUBINSTEIN Nathan Nuta, geboren am 23.12.1893 in
Partschew, letztbekannter Wohnsitz: Schaerbeek
(Brüssel) 26, rue Deloght, war vom 16. August 1942
von St. Privas (Ardeche) kommend, zum Zwangsaufent-
halt in der Festung Barraux bis 28. August 1942 und
wurde am 2. September 1942 vom Sammellager Drancy
zum KL- Auschwitz (Häftlingsnummer nicht angeführt)
überstellt.

At the war's end, I received this letter from the International Red Cross informing me that my father had been deported from the internment camp of Drancy on September 2, 1942 to Auschwitz.

With my mother in Basel, summer of 1946.

My love, Vera Polgar, skiing at a resort in the Western Alps during our spring break from the University of Basel.

Renee and I sign the ketubbah, *the Jewish marriage contract, on our wedding day.*

This monument on the outskirts of Jerusalem is dedicated to the memory of the Jews deported from France to Auschwitz. Here I found my father's name.

Celebrating Father's Day with my wife Renee, daughter Natalie and grandson Michael.

Chapter Nine

Camp Sierre

At the end of the week, the promised parcels of clothing arrived. I was glad to change into some new shirts and pants. Similar gift parcels, we found out, had been distributed at the women's camp.

On the following Monday, the commandant announced that a contingent of twenty men would leave for a work camp at Sierre, fifty kilometers inland. I was surprised to find my name on the list. I had hoped to stay close to my mother and see her on weekends. When I talked to the commandant he listened to my request, but turned me down. "The decision has been made," he said. "Nothing can be changed. You will like the place. It is a ski resort and after work, there will be leisure time in the village. Best of all, you will be paid for your work."

Our group left the next morning. I had been allowed to see my mother briefly. She was quite upset at the turn of events, but I promised to write often and make sure to obtain a pass to visit her. There was, however, one bit of good news. Marcel Stern was among the men selected. I would have a friend at Sierre after all.

An army truck took us through some truly spectacular mountain scenery; we passed picturesque chalets nestled along the road, partially hidden by trees in full glory of their fall foliage. For the first time since my arrival, I felt at peace with myself and was actually looking forward to a new experience.

After a couple of hours, the truck stopped in front of a row of barracks not unlike the ones we had just left, except considerably smaller. A stocky man in work clothes appeared and led us to our quarters. Four windows with white curtains brightened up the place. Plaid wool blankets were neatly folded on each cot and the back wall was covered with a large Swiss flag.

The man introduced himself as Bruno, the foreman, then proceeded to show us the adjacent shower facilities and the mess hall. Around noon we were served hot pea soup with pieces of meat and a slice of black bread. At the end of the meal, Bruno introduced a short, wiry man in his fifties. He wore civilian clothes and black boots. "This is Mr. Rodier," Bruno told us. "He is the director of the camp and will give you your instructions."

Mr. Rodier nodded, then addressed us: "You have arrived at a work camp where you will be doing useful and important work for the country that has taken you in. The work will be hard, but you will be treated fairly, as long as you follow the rules, are not lazy and do not create any disturbance. Remember, you are a guest here."

It was not the type of welcome we expected.

In the afternoon Bruno marched us to a nearby clearing where two workers handed out heavy boots that seemed all of one size. When I put on my pair, my feet were literally swimming in them and I had a hard time walking. I pointed this out to one of the men, but he paid no attention to me.

We walked along a narrow path to an area that was partially underwater. After handing us large shovels, they separated us into two groups. "These are swamps that need draining to construct logging roads," Bruno explained. He then used a ribbon to demarcate an area fifty feet long and thirty feet wide. "Your job is to create a four foot water level by hauling that muck out. Once that is done, we will pump the water into cisterns. Let's get started."

We stepped into the muddy swamps. The water came up to our kneecaps. We each were assigned a portion of that area and told to start digging. Raymond, a tall thin fellow from Antwerp was at my right, while to my left was one of the older men, Mr. Bromski, a watchmaker from Brussels.

I dug into the murky slush and tried to lift my shovel, but nearly toppled over. The weight of that soil was staggering. When I reduced the load by at least one half, I was able to go on, though my back felt like it was on fire after just one hour. I stopped and noticed that Mr. Bromski had sat down along the edge of the swamp, perspiration running down his flushed face. He was breathing heavily.

Bruno had disappeared, leaving one of his helpers in charge who spotted us. He came running and started to scream: "What the hell do you think you are doing? I did not tell you to stop working. We won't tolerate shirkers! Now let's go and I mean NOW!"

I kept on shoveling. Moving close to Mr. Bromski, I whispered, "Turn your back toward that bastard, so he can't see what you are doing. Just put a small amount of mud on that shovel and throw it over the edge."

After four hours without a break, a whistle was blown and we put down our shovels. I emptied my boots, which had collected water. My newly acquired shirt was covered with black soil and soaked from perspiration. My feet were swollen and full of blisters from rubbing against those much too wide boots. We ate our evening rations in silence and fell on our cots in utter exhaustion.

In the morning we resumed digging. Mr. Rodier had joined Bruno and his assistants and he watched us intently. He had brought along a measuring stick. Holding out his arm as far as he could, he lowered the stick into the water. "You have a long way to go," he told us. "You haven't even reached two feet. You better learn to work faster. We cannot afford to waste time!"

This routine went to for the next few days. We had found a way to beat them at their own game. The younger guys were digging along the perimeter about three feet from the edge. When Mr. Rodier came up with his measuring stick, he would find that his goal of a depth of four feet had been achieved. What he did not know was that in the center of that pond there was, directly under the dark, murky water, an area no more than a foot below the surface. This is where the older men had been digging. Eventually, we knew, our tormentors would get wise to that scheme, but for the moment we felt rather smug having deceived Mr. Rodier.

After several weeks we got a pass to go to the village. I placed a call from a phone station to the camp at Bex, but was unable to talk to my mother. A nurse told me she had been brought to the hospital for a checkup that morning. "She is doing fine, and has recuperated rather well," she added. I told her that I would try to call back.

The next day, Mr. Rodier came into our barrack announcing that our group was given a new assignment. We were elated. Whatever that new job was going to be, it had to be an improvement over our swamp ordeal.

We were driven in a pick-up truck to what appeared to be an abandoned railroad station. Three husky, heavy-set men were standing near a large shed. One of them approached us. "My name is John Eggeli," he said in a brusque voice, "I am the foreman." He opened the door to the shed and pointed to a number of railroad tracks, each about ten feet in length. "You are to take these tracks, one at a time, and bring them to a road marker behind the station. I will then instruct you what to do next."

Raymond and I walked over to the tracks and tried to lift one of them, but could not move it an inch. Mr. Eggeli started to laugh. "Not so fast. It will take the ten of you to move that track. I want you to line up, five on each side. Space yourself so that you are not directly facing each other. Next get a grip on the track. Count to three and lift it up at the same time. Then start moving sideways, very slowly, until you get to the marker. I will be right there to guide you."

This is how we lifted that steel monster, shuffling sideways, one foot at a time, our muscles straining to where we were ready to collapse, until we reached the road. We then lowered the track very slowly while Mr. Eggeli was shouting orders from the sideline, "Easy now, one . . . wait! . . . two . . . a little lower . . . three . . . NOW!"

None of us had ever experienced anything like it and we seriously contemplated running away from that slave camp. But we all stayed on. Over the next few days we learned to improve our grip and distribute our combined weight, while moving in complete unison. Though we had been given heavy gloves, they were soaked with blood by the end of the day.

By early November we had completed that stretch of railroad tracks that linked the old station to a new building under construction. I finally had succeeded in reaching my mother by phone but was unable to secure a pass to see her. I decided not to tell her about my ordeal.

She had recuperated from her attack and told me that families with children and some of the elderly and infirm were to be sent to the Guetsch, a former five-star hotel near Lucerne that had been converted into an internment camp for refugees. "I wish you could join me," she said. "I am going to speak to the officer in charge and explain to him that you would help look after me during my recovery."

I did not believe her plan would work.

A few days later, when Mr. Eggeli announced that our group would be sent to a different workplace in the German-speaking part of Switzerland, near Zurich, everyone's spirits rose. He produced a list and called out our names. When he came to me, he seemed puzzled.

"Apparently you will go to the Auffanglager Guetsch near Lucerne," he said. "Looks to me that you have gotten special treatment. The Guetsch is primarily a place for women and children now. Frankly, I don't understand it. Well, just be ready tomorrow at six in the morning. You'll take the train to Lucerne. Somebody form the Guetsch will pick you up at the station." He kept shaking his head in disbelief.

That night I called my mother to share the good news with her. She was happy that her efforts had paid off and that we would soon be together again.

Chapter Ten

The Guetsch

Before the war, the Guetsch had been one of Switzerland's most popular tourist spots. Perched on a plateau with the area's two mountain peaks, Rigi and Pilatus, in the background, it offered a magnificent view of the famous lake below, dotted with sail boats and excursion vessels.

A cog rail made the spectacular ascent in less than thirty minutes. It was a cold and windy November day when I took that ride. My mother was standing at the exit waiting for me, accompanied by a nurse. She hugged and kissed me with tears in her eyes.

"You got very thin," she remarked. "Did they work you hard?"

"Not too bad," I answered, biting my tongue.

At the hotel, she introduced me to a tall, friendly man in the uniform of a major who welcomed me and directed us to the dining room where lunch was being served. All internees were housed in the original hotel rooms, which were quite spacious and spotlessly clean. My mother shared her room with an elderly woman from Antwerp. Her husband too had been arrested in the roundup in August.

Many of the women were young mothers with small children. The men had recently been sent to work camps around Zurich.

In the evening, we finally spent some time alone, reliving our incredible escape and talking about the fate of my father and our hope to be reunited with him after the war. My mother had saved some of the recent papers and magazines for me. I had not done much reading at Sierre and was anxious to find out how the war was going.

I was dismayed at the latest news. The Germans had continued their drive into Russia and were close to Stalingrad near the Caspian Sea, taking a great number of prisoners. In Africa, Field Marshal Rommel stood at the gates of El Alamein, a short distance from the Suez Canal.

Even the news from the Pacific was disturbing. America had suffered a number of setbacks and was obviously still struggling to rebuild a war machine severely hurt by the Japanese sneak attack at Pearl Harbor.

Earlier this month, American troops had landed in Algiers, one of the French territories in North Africa. Germany's reaction had been swift. Declaring that this action by the Allies voided the armistice treaty they signed with Pétain, they marched into the Unoccupied Zone on November 11. All of France was now under the direct control of the Nazis and their Italian allies. Had this event occurred just a few weeks earlier, my mother and I would have been caught in that maelstrom and unable to escape over the mountains into Switzerland.

My spirits were lifted when I read that, just this past week, the Swiss government had decided to end that infamous policy of turning Jewish refugees back at the border and into the hands of the Germans. There had been an outcry by the Swiss public, after the liberal press had brought that shameful action to their attention.

The men at the work camp had been told that they would get a three-day pass every six weeks to visit their spouses. The first contingent was to arrive at the end of the month. In the meantime, there were only three other young men at the Guetsch. Lucien Berg and Martin Feldman were my age. Harry Goldberg at eighteen was a year younger.

We were assigned to kitchen duty, which consisted of carrying fifty-pound sacks of potatoes up from the cellar and a variety of other tasks. For six hours each day, we peeled potatoes and rutabagas, sliced carrots and apples for the two hundred camp residents, hauled milk cans and did any chore the cook, a heavyset army corporal, could think of.

After the evening meal and a short break, we were faced with unending stacks of dishes to be washed. The smell of dirty dishwater permeated everything we wore. Our hands wrinkled and we generally collapsed on our cots, too tired to take that much needed shower.

Usually in the morning, we would tend to our hygiene. After a week of that routine, I was wondering whether the Swiss made it their business to test just how much work they could load upon us. Then again, it beat lugging railroad tracks.

I became friendly with Harry, who was studying for his *baccalauréat* in every moment that he could find and was hoping to enter university. He had been able to get hold of some books he needed to prepare for the exams. Looking over his books, I became quite depressed. The consequences of having missed four years of schooling by taking the job at the Jewish Committee in Brussels and the war years that followed were now quite clear to me.

Though I had read a lot and was familiar with works by modern American, French and German writers, in addition to having taken some Berlitz self-taught language courses, there were gaping holes in my education.

My knowledge of algebra, trigonometry and calculus and anything to do with chemistry and physics was nil. Right then and there I decided that I must use the time waiting for the war to end, be it months or years, in a way that would fill those voids and prepare me to meet the challenge of the future.

I kept in touch with some of the men from the work camp who I met on their visits to the Guetsch. One of them, Walter Sperling, was a congenial fellow from Vienna in his mid-forties; his wife Irene had introduced us. He was an avid chess player and we spent many hours hunched over the chessboard. Walter had told me that the work at the camp consisted of cutting down trees and that while the work was hard, he was getting a decent pay in addition to a three-day pass to Zurich every six weeks.

He also informed me that some of the younger guys were using the evening hours to study subjects they needed for future job training. They even had been allowed to visit the Zurich library and borrow books relating to college admission preparations.

This was exactly what I had in mind. When I told my mother of my decision to join Walter, she was very upset at the thought of my leaving and engaging in the type of work she considered dangerous, but in the end she relented.

"Please understand that this is a wonderful opportunity, maybe the only one, to make up for all those missed school years," I told her. I promised to call her often and visit her as soon as my first pass came due. The next day I made a formal request for a transfer to the work camp of Bonstetten. To my great surprise, the request was granted immediately and within days, I was on my way.

Chapter Eleven

Camp Bonstetten

I boarded the train for Zurich full of anticipation, leaving behind lovely Lucerne with its fourteenth-century watchtowers and that famous covered bridge, Europe's oldest.

The scenery from my window was breathtaking. Valleys bathed in fall foliage alternated with snow-capped mountain peaks. Snaking through a number of tunnels, the train would emerge to ever changing vistas, one more spectacular than the other. For a brief moment, I dreamed I was a tourist on a holiday, rather than a refugee on his way to a work camp.

Zurich had that big city feel. It was my first encounter with a metropolis since we left Brussels three years ago. There was, however, no time to explore the place, since I had to catch a bus to the village of Bonstetten, my destination.

The camp was located about two miles from where the bus had let me off. I walked briskly along a dirt road and soon spotted a row of wooden cabins surrounded by birch and elm trees. The men in blue work clothes were swinging their pickaxes, chipping away at a large tree trunk, paying no heed to me. A stocky man puffing on a cigarette stood at the entrance.

"A newcomer?" he wanted to know.

I nodded. Pointing to a cabin door, he said, "Just ask for Richard. He's the foreman."

Richard, a big, broad-shouldered man with a long black moustache and bushy eyebrows, sat behind a desk smoking a pipe. I handed him my transfer papers. He seemed satisfied. "I'll show you to your quarters," he said.

The barracks were similar to the ones I had been in before. I wondered if the day would ever come when I would sleep in a regular bed, not an army cot, and in a room all by myself.

A young man was sweeping out the place. He was a friendly fellow who informed me that this was not a camp run by the army, like most of them, but by a Swiss civilian company that supplied timber to building companies. I inquired about Walter Sperling. I hoped that I would be able to work in his group. When I met the young man again at lunch, he promised to ask the foreman if I could be assigned to Walter's detail.

The foreman, however, denied my request. "You are a beginner," he said, "Walter is in the more experienced squad."

In the afternoon they put me to work. I was given an ax and told to cut large chunks of wood into smaller pieces. Though the work was tiring, I enjoyed being out in that fresh, cold air, swinging that ax with a vengeance. I was given a cap and gloves, with the rest of my work clothes to be issued in the morning.

Walter and I finally got together in the evening. I delivered a letter from his wife and brought him up on the latest news from the Guetsch. He told me that he was looking forward to visiting her at Christmas, in just a few weeks. "I have to pick out a nice gift for her birthday this weekend when I get my pass to go into town," he added. He then produced a chess set and we spent that first evening and nearly every evening that week playing our favorite game until it was time to turn in.

Walter was paired with a husky Russian by the name of Vladimir whose knowledge of German was very limited. They cut down trees with a giant saw, moving in perfect rhythm. Watching them, I wondered whether I would ever be able to do that kind of work.

When Walter got his two-day pass, he talked the foreman into giving me a pass too, even though as a newcomer I was not entitled to that privilege. We walked on the renowned Bahnhostrasse, Zurich's finest street, looking at the store windows of beautifully decorated shops loaded with exquisite merchandise, apparently for shoppers who could afford the steep prices.

I had to limit my purchase to a handkerchief for my mother. Walter selected a lovely coral necklace for his wife. "December 27 is her birthday," he said. "It's all I can afford. I hope she will like it." I assured him that she would.

Toward the middle of December, I got a pleasant surprise. My friend Harry Goldberg arrived from the Guetsch. After I had left, he too requested a transfer to the work camp, hoping to accelerate his studies by making use of the facilities offered by a big city. He was assigned to the cot next to mine. I was glad to have a friend my age in that place.

Christmas was just days away. A tall tree took up a large space in our mess hall. Trimmed with a multitude of colorful ornaments and sparkling lights, it put us in the holiday spirit while a loudspeaker brought us carols all day long.

It was in the early morning hours of December 21, just as Harry and I were loading woodcuttings on a wheelbarrow, when we heard screams coming from the direction of the tree cutting detail. Leaving our station, we ran toward the clearing. Within seconds men were emerging from all sides.

Richard was standing in front of a felled tree, waving his hands and screaming for a doctor. On the ground a man was lying face down and motionless in a pool of blood. Richard kept yelling, "Where is that damn medic?" Turning toward the men surrounding him, his voice trembling with emotion, he kept on blurting out the same words over and over: "When I called TIMBER, he just kept on running right into the path of that tree. Right into it! He had never done that. Never!"

A slender man with a first aid kit came running and bent over the fallen man. After a few seconds, he looked up and shook his head. "He is gone," he said in a toneless voice. I moved closer to get a glimpse. The medic had moved the man slightly and I was able to see his face. It was Walter Sperling.

My head started to spin. Harry tried to hold on to me, but I slumped to the ground. I made an effort to get up, grabbing Harry's arm. "No! No!" I screamed. "Oh my God! This can't be! Why Walter? Why him?" I turned to Harry, "Tomorrow he was supposed to go home to his wife. Did you know that?" Harry nodded. "And he had a present for her birthday. Who is going to give her the news?"

The ambulance arrived and took Walter's body away.

The camp director had put in a call to the Guetsch. A nurse was with Irene now. I asked him to let me call my mother. She was terribly shaken and barely able to talk.

"I was with Irene when she got the news," she told me. "The doctor gave her a sedative and she seemed remarkably calm. The realization of what happened had not fully sunk in. I wish you were back here and away from that terrible place."

A pall had been cast over the entire camp. Christmas came, but the Grim Reaper had made this a hollow day as we sat around talking in low voices, remembering a friend.

February brought one of the worst snowstorms in years, according to Richard who had lived in the area since childhood. For a few hours each day, we continued piling up stacks of wood and moving them to covered sheds, but soon all work stopped. We spent the time huddled around the two stoves that warmed the barracks, stoking fires, playing cards, or just lying on our cots, alternating reading and dozing off.

We also managed in some lively debates on every topic, from the conditions in our camp, to what kind of world we hoped to live in once the war had come to an end. I had gotten hold of an old Underwood typewriter and was pounding out single sheets of daily commentaries in French and German, the two languages spoken in the camp. I had some very definite ideas about the future of our youth that did not always meet with reader approval, which led to some heated discussions.

Among my "projects" for a better world was a plan to separate youngsters between the ages of ten and sixteen from their parental environment for periods of two to three years, providing community living for the youngsters and fostering a spirit of sharing and caring. I felt that parents had failed to provide such an environment and had thus contributed to the kind of world we had inherited. I suppose what I was proposing was in fact a combination of kibbutz living with a healthy dose of socialism thrown in.

Toward the end of the month, we received the visit of a high-ranking representative of the Swiss Red Cross. Mrs. Gertrude Kurtz was a tall, portly woman in her fifties who, we were told, made the rounds of a number of work camps the government had established for the refugees from Nazi persecution, checking out the conditions in each of them. After inspecting our barracks, she engaged in friendly conversation with the men, asking about their backgrounds and families. She seemed genuinely interested in learning as much as possible on this short visit.

She stopped at my bulletin board and, much to my surprise, spent a good amount of time reading my comments. Turning to the commander who had tagged along, she spoke to him briefly. The commander nodded and called my name.

Mrs. Kurtz, it appeared, wanted to talk to me. I must confess that I was somewhat apprehensive. Could it be that I had expressed some ideas too radical for neutral Switzerland? My worries turned out to be unfounded. She asked me to follow her to the commander's office where she made herself comfortable behind a large desk. Motioning me to sit down, she adjusted her glasses and gave me a big smile.

"This is quite a paper you are writing," she commented. "How old are you?"

"I am nineteen," I said.

"Tell me a little about yourself," she inquired. "Where did you live before the war? How did you get into Switzerland?"

I gave her a brief synopsis and she looked pensive. "What is the extent of your schooling?" she wanted to know. I told her that I stopped school at fifteen to help my parents in Brussels by taking a job as an errand boy at the Jewish Committee for the Refugees from Germany and Austria.

"You mean to tell me that you actually never went to high school?" she was genuinely surprised. "You write very well. Where did that all come from?"

I told her that I had always been an avid reader of anything I could get my hands on—books, brochures, magazines, newspapers. For a few moments she was quiet. Then she said, "How would you like the opportunity to finish your studies?"

"I would like that very much," I replied.

"I know of an excellent private school that specializes in preparing students for admission to the university," she continued. "Are you willing to devote one year to such a program? You would have to work very hard to make up all the missed years with little free time left for anything but your studies. You would receive a scholarship from the Red Cross that includes the cost of the private school as well as your room and board. And if you pass the *Eidgenoessische Maturitaet,* the very stringent entrance exam to the university, the grant can be extended to cover the tuition costs too. How does that sound to you?"

For a few moments I was absolutely speechless. A miracle was happening in front of my eyes. An angel had come to take me away from what I had accepted as simply the place to wait out the war.

"I don't know what to say," I finally replied. I had a hard time keeping from choking up. "I'm so very grateful for this incredible chance. I promise that you will not regret your generosity."

Mrs. Kurtz nodded and took my hand in hers. "I know you will do well. Do you know what subjects you would like to take up in college?"

"I was thinking of becoming a teacher of history and languages," I said.

"Good. That is a fine career choice." Then she added, with a wistful smile, "You can always write for newspapers on the side. But, first things first. The school is located in Basel. It is called the 'Athenaeum.' There is just one more thing." My heart started to sink.

"The courses have already started and the new semester begins in the fall," she continued. "You have therefore, the entire spring and summer to do something useful. We have a home for Jewish children who had been smuggled over the mountains from France after the arrest and deportation of their parents. The place is located in a small village called Speicher on the northeastern corner of Switzerland. I would like to send you there to assist the only teacher they have right now, Dr. Andre Klein, a chemist from Paris."

"But how can I teach when I have so much to catch up on myself?" I wanted to know.

"You will do just fine. The main thing is to have a person looking after these youngsters between the ages of eight and sixteen. They need help with organizing their daily chores, their homework and their leisure time. Dr. Klein is a very nice man and he will be able to help you. So, are you ready?"

"Yes, I am," I said. "I will do my best, I promise."

"Good. I will make the arrangements for your departure with the commandant. I will also give you a letter of introduction to Mr. Fischer, the director of the home."

"Is there a chance of seeing my mother in Lucerne before leaving?" I asked.

"I think we can arrange it." With that, she got up, shook my hand and gave me a big smile. "Good luck, Leon. I will be in touch with you."

The commandant was very gracious and promptly gave me a three-day pass to visit my mother. Word of my good fortune spread rapidly and everybody seemed happy for me, particularly Harry, who was preparing for the *baccalauréat*, the exam for graduation from secondary school which was required for admission to the university. We talked about possible places to meet once he knew which college he would attend.

Throughout the trip to Lucerne, I was excited at the thought of surprising my mother with this amazing turn of events. I found her sitting in a wheelchair in her room. She had slipped and hurt her back, but the nurse assured me that she was already much better and that there was nothing to worry about. She was filled with joy when I told her the news and wanted to know how far the place was and whether I would be able to visit her. I had forgotten to ask that question but I was sure there would be no problem.

A week later, I was on the train to St. Gallen, the city from which I would take the local up the mountain to Speicher.

Chapter Twelve

The Children's Home at Speicher

The little train chugged along at a leisurely pace, allowing me to savor the idyllic scenery with hills now nearly completely buried under thick layers of snow. Towering in the distance was the Mount Saentis, which at 6,732 feet was the highest mountain in northeastern Switzerland.

It was late in the afternoon when I arrived in Speicher. The stationmaster gave me directions and after twenty minutes of brisk walking in that chilly air, a wool scarf tied around my neck, I spotted the house on the very top of the hill. A massive, three-story building, it was surrounded by towering pines.

The road leading to the entrance had been swept clear of the snow that covered the meadow in front of the house. I put my small suitcase down and rang the bell. A middle-aged woman, her hair in a bonnet, opened the door. "You must be the new teacher," she said with a friendly smile. "Come on in. The director is waiting for you."

To say that I was nervous and apprehensive would be an understatement. After all, I had never taught before and I was barely three years older than the oldest student.

Mr. Fischer turned out to be a tall, broad-shouldered man in his forties with thinning hair and the beginning of a paunch. He shook my hand and guided me to a large hall where some fifty youngsters were watching a ping-pong game in progress.

The director waited a moment until he had the attention of the boys to introduce me. After acknowledging me by waving their hands, they promptly concentrated on the game again.

"Let me show you your room." Mr. Fischer said, opening a door at the end of a hallway. "You will share it with another teacher, Dr. Klein. He is in the village right now, but should be back for supper shortly. You can leave your suitcase in the room. Then he added, "Why don't you join the boys and get acquainted?"

Sitting on a high stool and apparently serving as a referee was a short blond fellow. He looked at me with a mischievous smile. "I am Maurice," he introduced himself. "Are you good at it?" he asked, pointing to the match in progress.

"Not too bad," I answered, not revealing that I had won several trophies back in Belgium.

The match ended with a tall, lanky guy apparently the winner, as his wide grin seemed to indicate.

"Henri here will play you," Maurice decreed with the demeanor of one used to making decisions. Henri, I was sure, was the school champ and I was being tested.

In the first set, Henri destroyed me. Some of the spectators started to move away from the table. During the second set, I pulled out all stops and managed to trounce my opponent rather decisively. The third set was a cliffhanger. Henri's reputation was at stake. The set lasted forever. Finally I managed to beat him with a score of 27–25.

Maurice looked at me. "You're O.K.," he said. I had it made.

When I entered my room. Dr. Klein was sitting on his bed. He was a handsome man of about thirty with an engaging smile that immediately put me at ease. "My name is Andre," he said. "Welcome to Switzerland's most remote village."

He had emptied out one section of the dresser to make room for the few shirts and shorts I had brought. "I have most of my things down in St. Gallen, where my wife and my two-year-old daughter have a small apartment. I see them every other weekend. I will introduce them to you."

Andre wanted to know all about me, how I got into Switzerland and where I had lived before the war. I started giving him a brief summary when the bell rang announcing dinner was being served.

The teachers, it turned out, ate in the kitchen with the other staff members, while the youngsters were seated in the hall where I had watched the game. The ping-pong table had been moved to the wall and a row of tables and benches now took up the space. Two of the boys were carrying large metal food containers and started to serve the meals to the group. I was surprised to see no staff in attendance, but decided not to say anything.

At the kitchen table, the director introduced me to the cook, Stefan, a lean blond Polish fellow, and his wife Anna, who worked in the kitchen and did most of the household work. Frau Weber, the woman who had greeted me first, was the manager. She took care of everything, seeing that the laundry was done weekly, that the rooms kept in perfect condition, and purchasing the needed supplies at the village grocery store.

Stefan, Andre explained, was also doubling up as the gardener and jack-of-all-trades. Twice a week a man from the village came up to do some wood-cutting and sweeping around the building. I was very much impressed, but remembered that this was Switzerland, where hard work was considered a national virtue. I wondered what Andre and I were expected to do besides teach. After a hearty meal consisting of the ever-popular polenta, this time a tasty corn dish with meatballs and a spicy sauce, with apple cider, pears and apples for dessert, Andre and I retired to our room.

There he gave me a complete rundown of what a day at Speicher consisted of including what our duties were. The boys, he told me, attended school in the village for only a few hours in the morning. The language was German and all the boys came from either France or Belgium. While they obviously were learning some German, the other subjects were not given the needed attention. This is where we came in. We were supplied with books and a curriculum for each grade with the idea of transforming some of this material into French instruction. Andre, who was a chemist by profession and had been working in a chemical plant near Paris, was given the task of teaching math and science, subjects in which he was very proficient. Since I spoke German fluently I was to help the boys with their daily assignments and at the same time go over such subjects as history, geography and French literature.

In addition, we were expected to assign their daily chores, make sure that good hygiene was maintained, that order and discipline were upheld, and above all, as Andre put it, to lend support and comfort to make the separation from their families more bearable.

The director, Andre confided, restricted his activity to spending long hours at his desk, most of it with a little glass of schnapps, so the rumors went, and occasionally reprimanding some real tough kids when everything else had failed.

Surprisingly, it took me no time to get used to the daily routine. One pleasant activity was early in the morning, before shower and breakfast, when we would don our skis and hit the slopes. It was a sight to behold, all these youngsters on wooden skis schussing downhill, barely avoiding the jutting trees and performing like pros though they just recently had been exposed to that most exhilarating of sports. I, too, got the hang of it in a very short time. Andre had been a skier for years and usually led us downhill. It was only after that invigorating routine that we were ready to start off the day.

Andre and I decided to engage the youngsters in subjects that were not exactly part of the curriculum. Andre started a calculus course. I introduced Plato, Descartes and Goethe. These out of the mainstream topics met with surprising enthusiasm. The more we threw at them, the better they liked it.

It was Maurice, though, whose razor sharp mind elicited a grudging respect from even the older ones. At thirteen he absorbed knowledge like parched earth soaks up the drenching rain after a long draught.

While their taste in music tended towards the loud and often discordant, I would surreptitiously move the radio knob toward the classical music station. Soon, like a modern Pied Piper, I started to attract a small group listening to Beethoven, Mozart and Brahms, with new recruits coming on board every evening.

Though some knew how to play chess, I decided to teach it to the ones who wanted to learn this fascinating game. Soon it became part of our weekly leisure activities. In no time, the boys were deep into brilliant openings, though the end games were tougher to master. As for Maurice, with his determination, bordering on stubbornness, he managed to draw me after some thirty games and finally beat me after fifty. It was his *jour de gloire.*

Most of the youngsters were from Paris and other large cities in France. A few came from Belgium and Luxembourg.

There was Henry, who excelled in all sports; Marcel, who never went anywhere without his harmonica; Alain, the comedian and pantomime specialist; Pierre, the quiet chess champion; and Camille, always smiling and ready to lend a hand.

Walter at seventeen was the oldest. He had fled to Belgium with his family just days before the Germans entered his native Vienna. They too had found refuge in the Unoccupied Zone of France. During the roundups, his parents were arrested and sent to the transit camp of Drancy near Paris. Walter, together with other young boys, was smuggled into Switzerland by members of the French Underground. Somehow he had managed to hold on to his prize possession, a violin given to him for his bar mitzvah and which he carried with him everywhere. Walter had learned to play the first movement of the Mendelssohn violin concerto and kept playing it with gusto every evening after supper. It was the one piece of music everybody soon was as familiar with as the "Marseillaise," the French national anthem. Strangely, all of them, as if by tacit agreement, would not talk about the one subject that surely must have been foremost on their mind: the fate of their families.

Both Andre and I refrained from prying, unless as sometimes happened during a nightly round, we would hear sobbing coming from one of the beds. Even then, we were careful to respect their innermost feelings.

Meanwhile we were encouraged by the news coming from the eastern front, where German forces had capitulated at Stalingrad on February 2. The Red Army apparently had taken the offensive after nearly eighteen months of bitter defeats.

During that same time, Allied raids over Germany intensified as well. Directly to the north of us was Lake Constance, which the Germans called Bodensee. The city of Constance was the base of the German dirigibles and was bombed nearly daily. At night the sky was one gigantic firework, fueled by continuous explosions, while on the ground, flames seemed to engulf everything. Waves of British bombers unloading their deadly cargo met with strong anti-aircraft fire and Messerschmitt fighters attempting to stem the assault.

The day attacks were even more graphic in their destructive furor. The heavens were covered with thousands of bombers, moving inexorably across the sky, forming a macabre carpet. Thick black smoke blanketed the town. Bursts of white clouds from the cannon fire of the batteries zeroed in on the Flying Fortresses, until a bulls-eye hit would send one of them hurtling down with a piercing, heart-chilling sound.

From the lawn in the back of the house, we had a front seat to Apocalypse. We watched, mesmerized, unable turn our eyes away. Miraculously the planes rarely strayed into neutral Switzerland and on the few occasion they did, caused little damage and no casualties.

One day, the rumor reached us that there was a way to find out whether any of the deported parents were still alive, by sending a card to a camp near Lodz, which the Germans had named Litzmannstadt. If the card came back with the stamp of the camp commander on it, we were told, it meant the person inquired about was indeed in that camp.

Henri volunteered to be the first one to send a card. The following month, it came back: It had the stamp on it! There was rejoicing and celebrating over the next few days and other youngsters rushed to send their inquiries to locate their parents and loved ones.

Returning from a trip to the village one evening, I found Andre slumped in a chair, his eyes closed. When I shook him gently he looked at me. In his hand was a card. He handed it to me. "The card is from the camp!" I exclaimed. "And the stamp is on it! You didn't tell me that you inquired about your father. Isn't it great? He is alive!"

For a moment, Andre kept silent. "My father died ten years ago in Budapest," he finally said in a toneless voice.

I did not immediately grasp the meaning of his words. When I did, I let out a scream: "Those bastards! Those goddamn lying bastards. It was all lies and deceptions!"

Andre whispered, "Let's not tell the boys. Let them have a little bit of hope." We never told them.

In the early spring, the director handed me two tickets for a concert in St. Gallen, which he was unable to attend. Andre had other plans, so I invited

Maurice to come with me. The famous pianist Arthur Schnabel was playing Beethoven's Emperor Concerto. During the concert, I would glance at my companion, wondering how he liked his baptism of classical music.

At the end of the concert and after a tumultuous applause, Maurice did not budge from his seat. His eyes were closed and for a moment I thought he had fallen asleep. When he opened them, he looked at me with a puzzled look, "That music . . ." he whispered, groping for words. "One moment my heart is filled with joy, the next one I feel like bursting out in tears and wanting to pray. I don't understand it." Ah, Maurice, a better description of Beethoven's music I never encountered.

In June, the soft, undulated landscape of green hills around us was in full bloom. Instead of skiing, we now engaged in the Swiss activity par excellence: walking. More precisely, we took long excursions to picturesque villages around the area.

Mr. Fischer, an avid mountain climber, decided to take us up the majestic Saentis on a Saturday. Because Andre and his wife were celebrating their daughter's third birthday in St. Gallen, the director chose me to be the other "mountain climb leader." I was not crazy about that decision. Memories of our perilous escape over the mountains the year before still haunted me. Mr. Fischer led our group of twenty; the others had decided to stay at the home.

After a couple of hours we took a rest and had our picnic. He told us that the next segment would be somewhat more "challenging": "From here on, the climb will become steeper and the path more uneven. I want you to follow exactly in my lead!" He then produced a heavy rope, fifty feet in length, and put one end around his waist. He told the boys to hold on tight to that rope and then, to my dismay, proceeded to tie the other end around my waist.

The idea, he explained, was for the two of us to be a stabilizing factor. It was not a very reassuring thought. I prayed that he knew that he was doing, because, as he was nearly twice my weight, if he were to miss a step we would leave this world together. Hopefully the kids would not hold on to their rope if such a doomsday scenario were to play out.

The higher we climbed, the foggier it got. At one point we could hardly see the person in front of us. A few of the younger ones started to cry. Mr. Fischer assured us that there was absolutely nothing to worry about, that this was one of the easiest mountains to climb in all of Switzerland and that he was an experienced climber who had climbed the toughest of them all, the Matterhorn.

After what seemed an eternity we finally got to the top. The view from it was stunning. The haze had disappeared. A vast panorama spread out before us; the Alps all around us, the Lake of Contance to the north, outlines of Austria, and even our tiny Speicher were visible to us. Mr. Fischer gave us a brief lecture about the area and its fauna before we embarked upon our return trek.

Somehow we were a little less apprehensive on the way down, even though the descent was not easy. The sound of cowbells preceded a herd of six cows led by a barefoot youngster who greeted us with a friendly *"Gruetzi"* as he passed us. We got back just before sundown, exhausted but at the same time, strangely exhilarated. We had become mountain climbers.

Shortly after, I had to take Maurice to the dentist in St. Gallen. We boarded the local train that made stops at every station. At the first stop, three Swiss soldiers entered our compartment, accompanied by a heavyset blond man in a washed-out khaki uniform. His pants were badly frayed and torn in several places. He was unshaven and dirty looking. I asked the soldiers who the man was.

"A Russian prisoner of war who escaped from a camp fifty kilometers from here," they answered. "We have one of them coming over the border almost daily. We are taking them to the post at Teufen for interrogation."

I had taught myself some Russian the year before and was anxious to try out my limited vocabulary. *"Dobraye Utra, Tovarich,"* I said. (Hello, comrade!)

"Dobraye Utra," he replied. He gave me a bright smile. Two of his front teeth were missing.

I pointed to myself and Maurice next to me and said: *"Yevrey"* (Jewish). Then I added, looking at Maurice, *"Mat i atyets deportansja"* (mother and father deported). Maurice listened intently as I translated for him.

The Russian's smile vanished. Slowly, he raised his outstretched right hand to his neck and then swiftly moved it across his throat several times. Maurice turned white as a sheet.

When the soldiers and the Russian got off at the next stop, I turned to Maurice, putting my arm around his shoulder. "What does he know?" I said quickly. Maurice pushed me away. His eyes brimming with tears, his voice shaking, he exclaimed, "They are all dead! I knew it. Everybody is dead! Dead! Dead!"

We traveled the rest of the trip in silence.

In May I was given a three-day pass to visit my mother at a rest home near the Guetsch where she had been sent after her fall. While she had not fully recovered, she was in good spirits and we spent the time bringing each other up to date.

She was anxious to know how my teaching experience had worked out and was pleased that things had gone quite well. I got permission to take her shopping in town. We found a lovely café overlooking the Lake of Lucerne and enjoyed some of those delicious Swiss pastries.

When we returned, I asked to speak to the director of the home. I told him that I was moving to Basel in the fall to attend a private college preparatory school and wondered whether it was possible to move my mother to that town, so we could be together again.

He explained that he was ready to discharge my mother from his place, but that it would be necessary to find a similar facility in Basel where she could receive the additional care she needed. He offered to do some research and promised to let us know as soon as he had located a place.

I thanked him for his kindness. We now had something to look forward to and I left in a very upbeat mood.

Just a few weeks later, an event took place that electrified all of Europe. On June 6, Allied forces under the command of General Eisenhower landed in France on the coast of Normandy. The Invasion we all had waited for, for such a long time, had finally arrived. We were glued to the radio, following every detail of the fierce fighting that was going on, the outcome of which would decide our own survival.

Around the middle of September, Mr. Fischer called me into his office. "I have somebody on the phone who wants to talk to you," he said with a dead-pan face. I picked up the receiver

"Hello Leon, this is Gertrude Kurtz." My heart started to beat faster.

"The time has come, my friend, to move on," she announced. "The fall session at the Athenaeum is starting next week. Mr. Fischer has all the information. Mrs. Brunner, our representative will meet you at the station in Basel. She is a very nice young lady who will help you with the transition. I will remain in touch with you. It is now up to you, Leon. Good luck!"

When I got back to my room, Andre was there waiting for me. He had gotten the news earlier. "I am really happy for you," he said. "I'll miss you. Stay in touch. When I return to Paris, which I hope will be soon, I'll stop at Basel and we will spend some time together."

That evening, when I walked into the dining room, all the youngsters and the entire staff were sitting at tables that had been decorated with flowers. A large banner had been strung across the entire room: *"Merci, Monsieur, et Bonne Chance!"* (Thank you, sir, and good luck!)

I was deeply moved and had a hard time not to choke up. After a delicious supper, Maurice approached me and handed me a small package. "This is from all of us," he said. I opened it. It was a gold chain with a Star of David attached to it. I was speechless. These youngsters had so little spending money and here they had given me that beautiful charm.

I looked around. Andre was waving at me. Mr. Fischer and his staff were smiling, waiting for me to address them. All the youngsters were suddenly very quiet.

"My friends," I said, "I cannot tell you what this gift means to me. I will always cherish it, remembering every one of you and the wonderful times we spent together.

"When I came here nine months ago, I was not at all certain that I would be able to live up to the task of being a teacher to some very bright students who were not much younger than I. You accepted me, you gave me confidence, and for that I thank you. Together with everybody in this room, Mr. Fischer, Andre and the entire staff, you all gave me the opportunity of learning my job, almost on a 'as you go basis.' If there is anything I take pride in, it has been your willingness to respond to my efforts to open doors to the beauty of the written word and the wonders of the world of the arts.

"Yet all these efforts would have been in vain had it not been for your insatiable thirst for more and more knowledge. As much as I tried to challenge you, you did the very same thing to me. It was your enthusiasm that made me want to pursue that most noble of profession, to be a teacher. As I leave Speicher, I am at once happy and sad. Happy to embark on a career that will fulfill me and enable me to continue the work started here, and sad to leave what has become a very important part of me.

"I wish you all the best life has to offer. Keep up your drive for knowledge and your exploration of the beauty of our small planet. Never lose your sense of curiosity. In spite of all the hardship and pain you have encountered in your young lives, never give up! Remember, our generation is the one that will be called upon to make this a better and more just world!"

Concluding my speech, I walked out of the door and back to my room. I did not want them to see me cry. After all, I was still their teacher for a while.

A few days later, Mr. Fischer told me that he would drive me to the station to catch the local to St. Gallen from where I was to leave for Basel, some two hundred kilometers to the west. I picked up my suitcase and walked through the door one last time.

Maurice was waiting for me. "Who am I going to play chess with now?" he wanted to know. "You are the only one who can beat me. It is going to be so boring!"

"You will be surprised," I laughed. "After awhile one of the younger kids will draw you and then one day, he will beat you, just as you did with me."

Maurice went over to me. Hugging me, he whispered: "You are going to write to me, won't you?"

"Of course, I will," I assured him, "and I expect to hear from you very often!"

"Oh, you will," he said. Turning around quickly, he went back into the house just as Mr. Fischer drove up.

Chapter Thirteen

Basel

As the train rolled into the huge station in Basel, one of Europe's largest, I was looking out of my window, straining to detect Mrs. Brunner, the lady who was supposed to meet me.

The platform was packed with people scurrying around and porters busy pushing carts stacked with suitcases. Children were crying, trying to hold onto their mothers. I had just about given up finding my contact when I spotted a young woman in a suede coat, wearing black boots, waving a large cardboard sign with just one word on it in big letters: L E O N.

Mrs. Brunner greeted me with a friendly smile: "Welcome to Basel, Leon. Mrs. Kurtz had asked me to take you under my wing. How was the ride?" I liked her immediately. Outside the station, she had a small Fiat waiting. "Let's stop for a cup of coffee," she proposed.

We spent the next half hour getting acquainted. I gave her a detailed description of my life in Switzerland, from our crossing the mountains and my labor camp experience to my recent stint as a teacher. She told me about her life as mother of a four-year-old and wife of an engineer.

"Now, let us turn to what is ahead," she said. "All necessary arrangements have been made to get you started without delay." She opened her purse and handed me an envelope. "This will cover your living expenses until next month, when we will mail you a check directly to your apartment. The place is small but cozy and only minutes away from your school. Dr. Mueller, the director, is expecting us in fifteen minutes. I will introduce you. As you know, the Red Cross is taking care of all your school expenses, tuition, books and materials. Any questions?"

I just shook my head. "I don't know what to say, Mrs. Brunner, I can never thank you people enough for all the help you're giving me."

"For starters, call me Anita," she said. Then, getting serious, she added: "We believe that you are worth the investment. So, work hard, Leon, and everybody will be happy."

Driving through some heavy traffic, Anita pointed out a large building. "This is the university, your ultimate destination. Very close to your school and residence." Moments later the car stopped in front of a small apartment house. "Here we are," she announced.

I was about to climb up the few steps leading to the entrance, when Anita stopped me. Pointing to another entrance below the street level, she said, "This is where your place is. It is called a *pied-à-terre,* another word for a cellar apartment."

Anita produced a key and we entered the place. The room was almost completely dark and after she had switched on the light, I was able to take stock of my new abode. The walls were covered with a bright yellow wallpaper that made the room appear larger. A double bed in the center was covered with a multicolor quilt. A table, two chairs, a stove and a small refrigerator completed the furnishings.

Opening a door, Anita said, "You even have your own bathroom. The folks on the upper floor must share it with other tenants."

"Where is the window?" I wanted to know. Anita pointed to a small opening directly below the ceiling. Looking up, I burst out laughing. A parade of legs was visible. Women's high heels alternated with bottoms of men's trousers. A baby carriage broke the monotony.

"I know," Anita nodded. "It takes a while to get used to it. Still, this is a convenient place, and reasonable. And you can always take a walk to see what is going on up there." I assured her that I had no problem looking at the world from that perspective.

The school building was located on a narrow one-way street. After we rang the bell, an elderly man opened the large wooden door and led us in. Anita introduced me to Dr. Mueller, a heavy-set man with dark bushy eyebrows and a stern demeanor. He scrutinized me while Anita gave him a brief overview of my educational background, pointing out the voids that needed filling.

Dr. Mueller nodded. "We will work out a plan that addresses your immediate needs, which obviously are math and the sciences. Mrs. Mueller, my wife, is in charge of these subjects. Her class is starting in ten minutes in room 201 down the hall. I will brief her about you." With that he dismissed us.

On the way out, Anita took me aside. "Don't be intimidated. Dr. Mueller gives the impression of a rough taskmaster, but he is all right. His wife is a whiz in math. You will see." Handing me a card with her phone number on it, she added, "Call me any time you need some help or advice. Good luck!" Then she was gone.

The classroom was spacious and well lit. Some twenty students were already sitting at their desks. A young woman motioned me to sit next to her, apparently the only vacant spot left. She had long flowing dark hair and a pale complexion. "My name is Yolanda Bianchi and I am from Milan," she said.

"I am Leon Rubinstein from France," I responded, shaking her hand.

At age 21, I had expected to be among the oldest students, but looking around I realized that the majority was my age or older. Obviously they were here to make up for lost time, just like me. The door opened and a tall woman dressed in a white jacket over a navy cotton dress strode in, her eyes sparkling. She greeted us with a hearty *"Gruetzi"* and immediately went to the blackboard. What followed then had us all in a trance.

Formula after formula appeared, letters and numbers intermingling endlessly. It was like watching a composer trying frantically to complete his masterpiece. Finally, when half the blackboard was covered, she turned around and smiling broadly at us said, "Is there anybody in this room who has any idea what all that means? If there is, he or she must leave at once. You already have completed the course." Then she added, "At the end of the school year, you will be able to come up here, analyze the problem and solve it, I promise you!" It was a fun beginning.

In a surprisingly short time, we were able to follow theorems, understand formulas, and memorize equations in our quest to master the mysteries of algebra. While apparently a few students had some knowledge in that field, she made sure not to leave anyone behind and I found myself strangely exhilarated as I entered the exciting world of mathematics.

The other subjects—English, French and German, as well as history, geography and the natural sciences—did not present any difficulties for me, and merely demanded my remembering certain facts and dates. This allowed me to devote the major portion of my study time to math, chemistry and physics.

During the next few months, I spent five eight-hour days at school, followed by at least three hours in the evening of going over the material in my small place below the surface of the city. The weekends were also a time for reviewing, although I allowed myself some relaxing time.

Mrs. Mueller shared the science lessons with another teacher, a young French professor, who tried hard to measure up to the standards Mrs. Mueller had set. While he could not keep up with her pace, he did his best to help us absorb the material. One day Mrs. Mueller called me into her office. "You are making good overall progress, but in math you have to be able to understand concepts," she said. "You have difficulties in thinking analytically. I have here a bunch of math tests that were given for the *Eidgenoessische Maturitaet,* the entrance exams for the university over the past ten years. Of course, you will not face the identical problems, but they will be similar. I want you to complete twenty tests a week, and we will go over the results. I believe this will greatly help you.

Indeed, that method of completing test after test and then have her go over the results, pointing out repeated mistakes and complimenting me on correct answers, seemed to work very well for me.

A few weeks after my arrival in Basel, my mother was transferred from Lucerne to a home for elderly women who needed some medical attention and where they were given room and board. The place was just minutes away from me. We both were very happy with the way things had turned out.

My diet consisted mainly of sandwiches and drinks, and only on weekends would I go to my mother's place for a home-cooked meal.

I found little time for leisure, but I did write to Maurice, who in turn kept me informed of daily life at Speicher. Dr. Klein was still there and no replacement had been hired to take my place. The hours at the school in the village had been increased as the boys became more fluent in German. "We miss you and your 'special fun lectures' on philosophy and music and of course, chess," he wrote me. "And yes," he added, "little Daniel, only eleven years old, finally beat me, as you predicted. It was a 'Black Day' for me!"

Among the students with whom I became quite friendly was Thomas, a very serious fellow of twenty-two who planned to become a doctor and hoped to go back to his native Holland after the war, and Yolanda, whose plans were still very vague. She confided that she had been engaged, but the fellow broke up with her at the last minute. This was one of the reasons she had decided to leave Milan where she was studying to become a nurse. The romance had seriously jeopardized her studies and she now had a rather hard time catching up with the basics that were required for a diploma.

The war, in the meanwhile, went well, though not with the speed I had hoped. After breaking through the German defenses in Normandy and freeing most of France, the Allies were now bogged down in the Ardennes, where the early snow, inclement weather and fierce resistance by Hitler's elite troops had brought the offensive to a halt.

After the liberation of Paris, we had expected an acceleration of the campaign that would lead to the collapse of the enemy. Now it looked as though we would have to go through yet another winter.

In the spring of 1945, the war finally came to an end. Our long nightmare was over.

Sadly, President Franklin D. Roosevelt was not to see the day of final victory. We all grieved for this great man, the savior of our continent. I remembered that sonorous voice, his messages to Occupied Europe that had sustained us all these years and kept our hopes alive. When he died at his summer retreat in Warm Springs, Georgia, he was only sixty-three years old. Days later, his nemesis, the cause of those twelve years of horror, Adolf Hitler, took his own life in a bunker below the rubbles of Berlin as the Russians were entering the city.

There was great rejoicing in the streets and although little Switzerland had managed to stay out of the war, everybody was celebrating the end of those long years of oppression. When the Allied troops entered Germany in the last days of the war, they had come upon a spectacle of indescribable horror, as they discovered a separate world within the collapsing Third Reich: the world of concentration camps, where ghostlike skeletons, barely alive, were begging for food, surrounded by piles of rotten corpses. A world of electrified wires and gallows, of gas chambers and crematoria. Millions had been murdered, men, women and children, the majority Jews.

Seeing the newsreels—our hopes dashed for a reunion, our hearts broken—we still went through the motions of contacting the Red Cross and other organizations to find out the fate of our loved ones. At night I would dream of a knock at the door. It was my father standing there, smiling and telling us how he had miraculously survived.

In August of that year, just two months before I was to take my exam in St. Gallen, we received a letter from the Red Cross. It contained the dreaded news.

My father had been deported from the camp of Drancy, near Paris, where they had sent him after his arrest in Aubenas and on September 2, 1942, he had been sent, together with over a thousand men, women and children, to a place called Auschwitz, the main killing fields of the Holocaust.

The same letter also told of the fate of my two cousins, Edgar, 14, and Leo, 10, and their parents, who were all sent to Auschwitz. Only a handful of people survived that hellhole on earth. No one of my family did.

I seriously thought of not going to St. Gallen. I just was too despondent. What kind of a world did we live in? Where was God when his children were being mercilessly murdered?

The next few days, I took long walks along the river and under the cool umbrella of trees that had already turned a reddish gold, and I thought of what lay ahead. I decided that I must complete what I had set out to accomplish. For my mother, in memory of my father and all he had taught me, and for myself. For the person I wanted to become—someone who would be part of that new world and help make it a better place for our generation.

On a chilly November day, I sat at my desk in a classroom in St. Gallen and started the week of oral and written tests for which I had worked so hard all year. Each evening we would compare notes. Mrs. Mueller, who had accompanied us, kept our spirits up by encouraging us and assuring us of her faith in our ability to tackle the challenges. Yolanda was depressed. She felt that she had done poorly. I tried to cheer her up as we sat down to dinner at the hotel where we were staying.

There were ten subjects in which we were tested: French, German, English, history, geography, the natural sciences, drawing, math, chemistry and physics. The maximum grade was 6. Two 2's would result in failure, no matter how good the rest of the subjects were. One 2 and one 3 were sufficient to pass. Of the hundred and twenty participants who had started out that week, only sixty-six passed. Thomas was the "Number One" student with a combined grade total of 56 out of 60. Yolanda failed. I came in sixth with a total of 50.

Although I had five 6's and three 5's, I nearly did not make it. My grade in physics was a 3 and in math, in spite of all the cramming, a dismal and nearly fatal 2. I guess a little luck did not hurt.

On the way back I tried to console Yolanda. I promised to help her prepare for next year's try, but she just shrugged her shoulders. "I think I'll go back to Italy," she said, sobbing and resting her head on my shoulder.

Later Dr. and Mrs. Mueller gave us a party at their place and I thanked them for all their help. "I guess I was not able to make a mathematician out of you, after all," Mrs. Mueller said with a hearty laugh. "But you did very well in your other subjects. What are you going to take up at the university?"

"I don't know," I said with a deadpan face, "Russian?"

"All right, wise guy," she replied. "What will it be?"

"Well, French, German, English. I like to teach languages. And history and geography and philosophy and . . ."

"Enough! It would take you eight years for all that. Well, you will come to a decision, I am sure. You have a good head on your shoulders and you are, as the French call it, a *débrouillard,* someone who is resourceful."

The following month, I matriculated at the University of Basel's department of philosophy.

That evening, my mother and I went to the temple. I said Kaddish for my father. And we remembered days long gone, but never forgotten.

As we were leaving the temple, a slender young man in his twenties approached us.

"You are Leon Rubinstein, aren't you?" I nodded.

"The son of Nathan Rubinstein?"

"I am."

"You don't remember me, do you?"

"Should I?"

"I was at the camp of Agde in the winter of 1940. Your father was the spokesman of the internees. He helped so many, including me, by contacting my father's sister in New York. I saw you saying Kaddish for your father. I am sorry. He was a wonderful man."

"Thank you for your kind words, Mister . . . ?"

"Joseph Bergmann. I have something else to tell you. Could we stop somewhere?" I pointed to a small coffee shop across the street.

The place was nearly deserted. After we had ordered some coffee, Joseph was quiet for a few moments. Then he cleared his voice: "I was together with your father at Fort Barreaux, the prison where they sent us after our arrest. They had picked me up at my home in St. Privas, a town close to Aubenas, that morning of August 20. I recognized him immediately and reminded him of our encounter two years earlier."

"But how come . . ." I started, when he interrupted me. "How come I am here today?" he responded. "That is what I want to talk to you about."

"When they brought us to that temporary detention place, I got friendly with a French guard who admired my gold watch, a gift from my grandfather. I told him that he could have it if he would help me get out of that place. He agreed. After I had seen your father, I went back to the gendarme and told him there was one more person I wanted to take with me. He first objected, but finally agreed and we set a time for the following evening. But when I told your father about my plan, he absolutely refused to come with me."

"But, why on earth?" I exclaimed.

"He just told me that he did not know where his family was. He would not be able to locate them, as they surely had been arrested too. To run away without papers or any money would only result in his being arrested again and perhaps severely punished. 'God willing,' he told me, 'we will meet again after the war.' No amount of pleading could make him change his mind. I assured him that we would join the Resistance—which I ultimately did—but it was all to no avail. He embraced me and wished me well. The following night, I escaped alone. I am sorry."

My mother grabbed his hand. "Thank you for telling us. And thank you for what you tried to do."

We walked home in silence. In front of her apartment, she turned toward me and asked, "Do you think your father would have entered that German limousine?"

She did not expect me to answer that question, and I did not.

Chapter Fourteen

Vera

College turned out to be a complete reversal of the assiduous and strict way I had approached studying all throughout the year. It seemed as if I had nothing but spare time, even though I made sure to attend all lectures.

After consulting with a placement counselor, I decided to specialize in French literature as my main subject for the first semester, with German and English as additional choices. I was not completely sure that I wanted to pursue a teaching career; journalism seemed attractive too, especially since I had a few articles published in leading Swiss newspapers over the past year. Obviously the mastery of three languages would come in handy whatever my final decision.

Going to America was still our goal. We had been told that our status as war refugees would make granting a permanent residency in Switzerland most unlikely. Returning to Belgium did not seem a very attractive alternative, as we had spent four years in that country waiting for the American visa. We renewed our correspondence with our cousins in Miami, who promised to send us the needed affidavits.

On a lark, I did take a beginner's course in Russian. A friend, Frank Gottschalk, whose mother was residing in the same place as my mother, had talked me into it. As a pre-med student, he felt he needed a diversion, and besides, as he put it, "Now that the Soviet Union has become a superpower, we all might need to speak Russian one of these days."

Madame Ostrowa was the quintessential "babushka," a Russian grandmother. All she needed was a scarf around her head. Shuffling in for the first lesson, dressed in a peasant blouse and dark print skirt and wearing heavy black hi-top laced shoes, she plopped herself behind her desk. After fiddling with her glasses and arranging some papers, she finally addressed us in a barely audible voice. She must have been close to seventy and I suspect we all were taken a bit aback, though there was also a feeling of compassion for that little old lady. Actually, we did learn the Russian alphabet and a folk song, which was a real accomplishment considering her rather limited singing ability.

Both Frank and I quit the course before the end of the semester. I am sure Madame Ostrowa was hurt by our defection, but we simply had enough of Russian culture.

Antisemitism did not end with the Nazis' defeat. Of the six million Jews who were murdered, three million were Polish Jews. The few among the survivors who decided to return to Poland were greeted with hatred and violence. In the town of Kielce, formerly the home of 15,000 Jews, 200 had returned, most of them waiting to immigrate to Palestine. When a Christian child disappeared the townspeople accused the Jews of having abducted the child so that his blood could be used in a satanic ritual. A wave of deadly antisemitic violence was unleashed resulting in the murder of 42 Jews before the child, who was at a friend's house, had been found. Similar incidents of violence against returning Jews were reported in other parts of Poland.

Of the 250,000 Jews who had become displaced persons after the war, most hoped to start a new life in Palestine. The British, who held the mandate of Palestine, had set up strict quotas and refused to ease any restrictions. Illegal immigration, with the help of Jewish underground agents, resulted in the arrival of some 70,000 people on the beaches of Palestine who came on rickety ships that dodged the British blockade. Discovery meant arrest and internment on the island of Cyprus.

Meanwhile at Nuremberg, the perpetrators of the greatest crime in history, twenty-four of the most significant Nazi leaders—those who had not escaped justice by committing suicide like Hitler, Goebbels and Himmler—were sitting in the dock, awaiting trial for crimes against humanity.

It was not easy for me to concentrate on my studies with the world in turmoil. I met students whose views of the future Europe were strongly influenced by the Soviet model. I also attended lectures by prominent Zionists who exhorted the young men and women in the audience to help build a homeland for the Jews. Still, my determination to immigrate to the United States was unshaken.

It was on a pleasant June afternoon when I first met Vera. I had left one of my courses and was strolling on the grounds of the university toward a small park nearby, where I intended to enjoy some quiet moments sitting on a bench, daydreaming. As I passed the music pavilion, I heard piano music coming through the open window. I recognized immediately the rhythmic figure used again and again in the first movement of Beethoven's best-known sonata for piano, the "Moonlight Sonata."

I walked up to the entrance. The door was slightly ajar and I stepped inside. The hall was rather small with empty chairs facing the stage. At the piano, her back turned toward me, sat a young woman, her long auburn hair covering her shoulders. She seemed totally absorbed as her fingers were caressing the keys, bringing forth the master's music with tenderness and a surprising maturity.

For a while I just stood there, strangely moved by that rendition of one of my favorite sonatas. Suddenly she stopped. Turning around and spotting me, she gave me a big smile, apparently not troubled by my presence. She waved me to come forward. As I walked up to her, she stretched out her hand: "My name is Vera Polgar."

I was rather surprised by her friendliness, since I had clearly interrupted her. She was a beautiful young woman, perhaps twenty years old, with big sparkling aquamarine eyes, full lips and pearl white teeth. Her rosy complexion told me that she liked the outdoors. I introduced myself and complimented her on her performance. "Are you a music major?" I wanted to know.

She shook her head. "No, this is a hobby now. I used to study the piano when I was small. My parents had great hopes for me, but things turned out differently. Now I am studying agronomy."

"But you truly play beautifully. It would seem a terrible mistake not to pursue a career in a field in which you obviously have attained a remarkable level of excellence."

"Thank you for your kind words. Sometimes circumstances in life result in having to make decisions that lead to a complete change of direction." She got up and closed the piano. "How about having a cup of coffee? That is, if you are free right now?" she asked.

"Great idea, I don't have any more classes today," I agreed.

We walked through the park along a fountain surrounded by beds of pansies in full bloom. She pointed to a small coffee shop off the campus area and for the next two hours we engaged in one long conversation covering every topic from school, to our future and the political shape of the world we inherited. I told her of my decision to become a language teacher and immigrate to America.

And we talked about the fate of our families. Vera's parents had lived most of their lives in Budapest where her father was a cardiologist. Her mother had been a member of the Symphony Orchestra's string section. After the takeover of Austria by Hitler in 1938, Dr. Polgar became convinced that war was inevitable. He sent Vera, his only daughter, to Switzerland where he had a cousin who took her into his home. Vera shared a room with the man's daughter, who was Vera's age. They went to private schools, learned French and perfected their German.

When the war broke out, Dr. Polgar was in the middle of negotiating the sale of his practice. After the Nazis' initial successes on the Eastern front, the Hungarian fascist party gained considerable strength and antisemitic actions multiplied. Dr. Polgar, who had been active in the Social Democratic Party before the war, was arrested. He had previously transferred monies to his cousin in Switzerland for the continuation of his daughter's education.

Vera's mother continued writing to her, keeping her informed on what was happening. She wrote that she hoped to be able to "visit" Vera. Soon thereafter, the deportations started and all mail from Hungary stopped.

For the next year and a half, Vera tried desperately to find out the fate of her parents. It was only at the end of the war that she learned that both parents had been on one of the last transports to Auschwitz, organized by Adolf Eichmann in his determination to send all Jews to their death, even as the Third Reich was collapsing.

Looking at her watch, she shook her head in disbelief. "You almost made me miss my next class, Leon. I must run now!" Scribbling a number on the back of an envelope she said, "Call me tonight. I'll be home by eight o'-clock." Then she was gone.

I was in a complete daze. Never before had I had a feeling of such immediate attraction. It was something that simply does not happen, and yet, here I was, filled with an inexplicable joy at the thought of hearing her voice later that evening.

From then on, our talks continued until late into the night. Over the next few weeks we spent every free moment together. We took walks and attended political lectures, spanning the range from the extreme left to the extreme right of the Zionist spectrum. We enjoyed concerts and movies and an occasional night on the town ending in a club, dancing until the early morning hours.

Suddenly all the routines I had adhered to faithfully, preparing for lectures, going to seminars, working on papers, seemed merely an interruption, albeit a necessary one, to my being with Vera. I could not remember having ever been as happy.

My visits to my mother became less frequent. When I told her that I had met a wonderful girl and that I was very much in love, she nodded. "I guessed as much. You seemed to be in a dream world lately. Who is she? Where is she from? Is she a student?"

"I want you to meet her." I said, "You will like her."

"Bring her over next weekend. I'll have some goulash and spaetzli for her. That will remind her of her native Hungary."

Vera and my mother hit it off immediately. Vera's vivacious personality, her spirited and animated conversation seemed to have a surprising stimulating effect on my usually reserved and quiet mother. Vera could not thank my mother enough for the homemade meal that brought back happier days. As we left, my mother embraced her and asked her to come back again soon.

"Only if I am doing the cooking next time," Vera replied. "And yes, I am a pretty good cook."

Vera had a roommate, Sylvia, a medical student from Geneva who had transferred to the University of Basel where her boyfriend was a language instructor. When I brought Vera home that evening, the apartment was empty. Sylvia had left a note on the kitchen table: "Stefan and I are going to Geneva over the weekend. There is plenty of food in the refrigerator. Have a good time." We looked at each other. Smiling at me, Vera pulled me toward the bed. We stretched out, cuddling in each other's arms, just savoring the closeness of our bodies.

We knew that what was about to happen would change our lives and seal the incredible miracle of our love. We explored and relished every step with no undue hurry. There was spontaneity to our lovemaking as we abandoned ourselves to the moment.

When I awoke in the morning with that lissome, ravishing beauty sleeping so peacefully at my side, my eyes were brimming over as I remembered that fateful encounter at the music pavilion only a few weeks earlier. When she opened her eyes, Vera put her arms around me. "I love you so much, *mon amour,*" she whispered.

"And I love you. I never imagined I could be filled with so much happiness." The sun shone through the window as we watched a flock of small white clouds chasing each other and felt our souls merging that Sunday morning.

After her roommate returned, we spent most nights in my little place that she called that "quaint catacomb." Gradually we went back to the normal rhythm of studying and meeting with friends whom we had neglected.

Vera was in her last year at the university preparing for her degree in agronomy which, she explained to me, would make her an expert in the science of managing farmland and improving crop productions—skills very much needed in the future state of Israel. Although she was a year younger than I, she was way ahead of me in her studies, since I had lost so much precious time.

Sooner or later, we knew, a topic would emerge that might well put a damper on our happiness. "Let's go to Palestine," she said one day. "We will get married under a cedar tree near the blue waters of the Mediterranean. We will help build a Jewish nation. Our children will grow up in a place of their own, never to be chased again!"

"You know that I have plans to go to America. That is where we have family. Why don't you go with me to that new world?" I asked.

"Leon, why would you want to go to America? Your family only knows you from your letters. You were denied entry all those years when your lives were in danger. Remember what you told me, it was the American consul who refused to issue the visa that could have saved your father's life!"

For a moment I was quiet. "America is a land where everybody has a chance to succeed if he is determined to work hard. After all, we have had nothing but a life of utter misery. Times of living in abject poverty, followed by years of running and hiding when we were in constant fear for our lives. Are we not entitled to a better life, one without a never-ending reminder of that terrible past?"

Vera looked thoughtful. Then she shook her head. "Maybe over the next few years, you will be able to build a future that will give you the material rewards you apparently are longing for. But what about over our lifetime? In the new state of Israel, we will be part of a beginning, a renewal of the Jewish soul. A vindication of what has been done to our people. Building a nation, brick by brick, making the soil fertile, seeing our children grow up to become proud and happy members of a new world—isn't that worth more than pursuing a dream of accumulating wealth?"

The debates would end there and we returned to our respective places, our hearts suddenly heavy.

When Vera asked me to accompany her to a Zionist meeting, I agreed. I found myself strangely moved by the enthusiasm, the energy and the unwavering optimism of those young men and women. They knew that they were facing hard times, not only because of the enormous task of building a nation with few natural resources, but also because they knew that the Arabs would not tolerate a Jewish state in their midst.

I had written to my cousins, reminding them to speed up the process that would enable us to get that long-awaited visa. They assured me that they were doing whatever was needed, but had been told that the quotas given before the war might no longer apply. Congress was considering placing some of the displaced people, now in holding camps, ahead of former applicants.

Gradually, I found myself embracing the thought of going to Eretz Israel with Vera. It was less out of idealism than the fear of losing her. When I told her of my decision, Vera embraced me with tears in her eyes.

"I prayed so hard, my love. We will be happy, I promise you."

"I have not told my mother yet," I said. "I wonder how she will feel about it."

"She will be happy, I am sure. I love her. She will be the mother I no longer have. And she will look after our children," she added with a wistful smile.

When I told my mother of my decision, she was very still. Her face was pale and there was a fear in her eyes. "What happened to our plans to immigrate after all these years of waiting? We have our family in America, the only ones left, and they are anxious to help us. Why can't Vera join us? I am sure she can find in America a way to help in the building of a Jewish state. Why after that terrible war, would she want to live again in constant danger and under the most trying circumstances?"

"Vera could not be happy in America," I said. "She strongly believes in the cause of Zionism. It is part of who she is."

"Can you be happy there?" my mother asked me.

"I will be happy where she is. I cannot think of a life without her."

My mother nodded. "Leon, this is a country for the young, for the builders, the pioneers. It is not a country for the old ones like me."

"First of all, you are not old. Furthermore, Vera wants you very much. She loves you. You have become a mother to her. And, as she told me, the future grandmother of our children."

My mother did not reply for a while. "Oh my dear boy," she finally said haltingly, "I will do whatever makes you happy. If it is going to Palestine with your love, and you want me, then I will go too. I don't know whether I will be able to master the language but you can always translate for me, can't you?"

Vera and I kept attending meetings at a friend's house discussing the possibility of going to Palestine on one of those illegal immigrant ships that were challenging the British blockade. The *Theodor Herzl* was supposed to leave for Haifa in the spring of 1947 and Jacob, Vera's mentor and the one who was the apparent contact with the organizers of that venture, explained in detail how we were to proceed.

Jacob was a short, broad-shouldered man in his late twenties with a slight limp he incurred at the Mauthausen concentration camp quarry in Austria when a large stone he was lugging fell on his foot. He had an engaging self-assurance and the ability to clearly outline the steps to be taken to accomplish our mission.

During the spring break, the Swiss authorities, under the direction of the central committee of the "Aid to Refugees," organized a combination study and vacation week for some fifty youths between the ages of eighteen and twenty-five. The young people had been invited from all parts of the country, from work camps, homes and cities. It was, as they put it, an experiment to bring together young people with different backgrounds and upbringings and have them work and play together. Above all, the organizers hoped to familiarize them with the challenges that a world left in shambles was now facing.

To our surprise all three of us, Jacob, Vera and myself, were among the select group of students invited to that conference. The place chosen was the resort town of Montana, one of the loveliest spots nestled high up in the Western Alps. There, at the Hotel Victoria, we attended meetings and talks spanning the spectrum of political diversity, from "Christianity and the Social Question" by a leading member of the clergy, to a discourse on "What Do We Bring to the Future?" by Fritz Wratenweiler, a well-known pedagogue. Other topics covered included "The ABC of Economics," "Ethics and Politics" and "Social Aspects of the Bible."

Questions of career choices, emigration, the building of a Jewish state, and the question of communism and socialism versus capitalism were all debated with fervor and conviction, though there were considerable differences among the participants. After all, we were representatives of so many factions—Holocaust survivors, Polish and Russian former prisoners of war, Swiss friends who wanted to give support, and even young Germans anxious to make amends for the sins of their fathers.

I was given the task of summarizing the week in a series of articles that were to be printed on a hand press and distributed to all who attended the event. All sessions took place in an amphitheater usually reserved for performances.

Without a doubt, it was the final speaker, Dr. Kautski, a writer and teacher who had spent six years in concentration camps—from Buchenwald and Dachau to Auschwitz—the sole survivor of his family, who left the most dramatic and deeply moving impression on all of us. I shall never forget that speech, though it was really not a speech, but a series of answers given haltingly, almost reluctantly to questions posed by the audience of the young who wanted to know the how, the when, and above all, the why.

"I am standing here, in front of you, and you are asking me to tell you what it was like in that hell on earth—you were a witness—so talk! But I cannot. I cannot because I do not possess the words. All the vocabulary I have ever accumulated is of no use. They are just sounds. They have no meaning."

A young man, perhaps eighteen, raised his hand. "Tell us, I beg you. Speak to us. I must know. My father was where you were. Please tell us what it was like."

Dr. Kautski looked at him. "How can I describe standing on roll call for hours that would not end, day and night, hands and feet numbed by a cold that cut through you like a knife with only one thought left: Not to fall down. Falling down meant the immediate dispatch to the gas chambers. Or when you attempt to sleep on rotten straw in those rat-infested, unheated barracks, trying to stay alive by pressing your freezing bones against the body next to you, only to awake in the morning to find that body cold and stiff, his journey ended. And your only thought is to take possession of his shoes?

"How can I define the smell? That pervasive, unending nauseating, sweet smell of death mixed with the smoke belching day and night from the chimneys. How do I explain the hunger, that constant companion that gnaws your inside to where the thought of a morsel of anything becomes an unbearable obsession? Above all, how can I express the overwhelming despair that surrounds the mind when thinking of the fate of those you loved and who loved you?

"Nor is it possible to give an account of the ones who simply have given up, who struggled no more. A species evolved in the world of extermination camps: the 'Musselmen,' as the S. S. called them, ghost-like inmates with no recognition of their environment, no awareness of themselves and no reaction, not even to inflicted pain. Eventually, those emaciated bodies simply would sink to the ground, lying motionless, like a bundle of discarded rags. As you see, my friends, there are no words left."

For a long time, we sat in utter silence. Our souls were aching as we reached out to the person next to us.

When we walked out of the hall that night, we all felt a deep responsibility to work together to make this a better world so that humanity never again will know the unspeakable horrors of those days.

The organizers of the conference insisted that, after all that hard work, we partake in sports activities. This meant rushing into the bracing air, tempered by the midday sun, donning our skis and schussing down the snow slopes while trying, not too successfully, to emulate our Swiss instructors.

The only fly in the ointment was the sleeping arrangements. I had to share a bungalow with two students from Holland, while Vera was put up in a room with two girls from Poland. "Sorry, my dear boy," Vera said with a mischievous grin, "you will just have to concentrate on our lectures and nature."

I suggested a little side trip to the village of Vermala, with a possible stop at one of those lovely country inns Switzerland was famous for, but she just shook her head. "The rest will do us some good. The week will be over soon," and with that she kissed me on my cheek—and zooming down the main piste, she soon disappeared from view.

In the evening we went dancing to Glenn Miller tunes in a night club, "La Petite Boite," holding each other tight, barely able to move on that crowded floor.

Upon our return to Basel, Vera was very busy preparing for the final exams. I had to catch up with some of my workload. Over the next few weeks we saw each other only on weekends. For my birthday, Vera had arranged to take my mother and me to a nice Viennese restaurant. After we dropped my mother off, we went to my place. Vera seemed quite preoccupied and when I pressed her, she told me that Jacob had made arrangements to have our group leave for Palestine on the *Theodor Herzl* within two weeks.

"We must immediately get started with preparations. We are boarding from Genoa. The voyage will take five days and we land by night. That is all I have been told."

"But that's impossible," I exclaimed. "How about your exam and my class schedule? Isn't there a way to postpone that trip for at least a few more weeks?"

She shook her head. "Jacob told us that this is our only chance, perhaps the last one for a long time, as the British have announced that they would enforce the embargo with all means at their disposal." Then she added, "Look, my love, we will be able to finish our studies in Eretz Israel, even if it takes longer. They have a top-notch university in Jerusalem and as soon as we arrive we'll get married. The Jewish Agency is going to help us with financial assistance and housing. We shall combine work and studying. It will be wonderful!"

"I guess I better tell Mother to get ready. I am sure she did not expect to leave that soon."

Vera looked at me with a strange expression. For a while she did not say anything. "Your mother won't be able to accompany us on this trip," she finally said. "It is a voyage fraught with all kinds of hardships and dangers. Only young people will make the journey. These are the instructions."

Then she added quickly, "Your mother will just have to wait a few more months. I am convinced that the British will lift the embargo in response to international pressure. As you know, the United Nations now has a definite plan for the partition of Palestine and the creating of a Jewish state. Once that becomes a reality, the doors will be wide open. Your mother will be with us before the end of the year, I promise!"

I sat at the edge of the bed, looking at her in disbelief. "You expect me to tell her to stay here in Europe, all alone, waiting for the day that she can join us, if and when that day arrives. It will break her heart."

"Please Leon, all that is asked of her is a little patience. She is in a good home here, with the Jewish Committee taking care of all her needs. She is a very intelligent and wonderful woman. She will understand the situation, you'll see. And she will be with us in no time!"

That morning we parted in silence. My heart was heavy and filled with sadness. When I told my mother, she did not respond. She had been folding some laundry, and kept on with it, without looking up. When she finally spoke, she sounded tired.

"I think Vera is right," she said. "This is a country for the young. You are both so very much in love. I understand it. This is your future."

"But you will be with us in just a few months," I said, perhaps not too convincingly.

She gave me one of her sad smiles. "It is all right. I will contact our cousins and they will send me the papers, just in case that dream of a Jewish state may not come about as fast as you both hope." Then she started to cry. I took her in my arms, but nothing would stem her tears.

Early the next morning, Vera called me. She had made an appointment with the regent at the university to inform him of her leaving. "Can you meet me around noon at my place?"

When I arrived, she was sitting on her bed, sorting through books and term papers. She got up and hugged me. "They were really shocked at my leaving before getting my degree. They actually tried to talk me out of it. I told them that this was an emergency and I was leaving Switzerland. They did not probe any further and wished me good luck." Looking at me quizzically, she said, "What did your mom say?"

"She said that she understood. Apparently she has resigned herself to staying here."

For a few moments Vera did not say anything. Then she nodded. "But you have not, have you?"

I took her hands and held them tight. "I cannot leave her here alone. Please understand me, my love. After all we have gone through together, the years of running from one country to another, the deportation of my father and his not coming back, our escaping, supporting and helping each other, trying to survive, hiding and in constant fear of being caught, until we finally arrived here. She is not a well person, as you know."

"What about us? What about our lives and our hopes? Do they not count for anything? Do you want to give it all up, our future and our plans? Leon, we found each other. I have never been so happy in my life and I know you love me. Can't you go along with our plan to have her follow us in just a few months? The time will go by so fast and we will be in touch with her all the time."

"Vera, I love you with all my heart. I cannot think of a future without you, but I also can't change who I am. Try to understand me. I will join you with my mother in just a short while, when we will be able to travel together to Palestine."

Vera shook her head. "No. You won't." She let go of my hands and sat down at the edge of the bed. "After a while, you will miss me less, our days together and the memory of those hours of happiness will slowly fade away. Oh, my love, don't you see it?"

We hugged and kissed each other, not wanting to let go, unable to stop our tears. When she finally got up, she said, sobbing between each sentence, "We are boarding in four days. I will call you the day before. Please leave now. It hurts too much. Stay well, my love, I shall never forget you. Never!"

That evening I walked aimlessly through the streets until the early morning hours, barely aware of my environment. My heart was filled with an overwhelming sense of sadness and despair. In my mind I replayed our last moments over and over again, and I knew then that Vera was right. I had made a choice and for now, we would go our separate ways.

When I told my mother of my decision, she struggled to express her conflicted feelings. "I do not want to stand in the way of your happiness," she said. "I would never forgive myself. Eventually you will regret that you gave up the love of your life. As you said, it won't be that long before I would join the two of you."

"Vera is leaving in a few days. Perhaps we will both join her once the state of Israel is a reality. Until then, I will stay in touch with her and I will go on with my studies."

Vera did call the day before her departure. She sounded composed and let me in on all the last minute details. Jacob and his friends had found a truck driver who would get them into Italy and bypass both the Swiss and the Italian border authorities. "I'll write to you from Genoa and when we arrive in Eretz Israel," she said. "God bless you and keep you. I love you."

It would be four weeks before I received a card from her. It was postmarked Haifa. She wrote that the voyage had been hectic as they had encountered bad weather and the ship had to make a detour to avoid a British navy patrol.

"The countryside is magnificent," she added. "The beaches along the blue waters of the Mediterranean are incredibly beautiful. Above all, the people are wonderful. Everybody is helping the newcomers to adjust to a new life. We have been given temporary shelters and some financial help. In a few days we will join a kibbutz, Ein Charod, not far from here. I'll write again very soon. I hope you and you mother are well, I love you so much! Your Vera."

Chapter Fifteen

A Nation Is Born

The weeks after her departure were sheer hell. Not having Vera in my life, not being able to hug her, to bury my face in her shiny long hair, smell the sweet scent of her soft skin and laugh at her jokes, deeply depressed me. I stopped going to classes, sleeping day and night. I blamed myself for having made a choice that would deprive me of a life of happiness.

My mother was saddened, seeing me so despondent. "You can still join Vera," she told me. "I will be just fine. I have friends who will look after me. And as you both had originally planned, I'll follow you once there is a Jewish state."

I shook my head. "We will make that journey together."

That night I sat down and wrote a long and passionate reply to Vera, assuring her that we will be together real soon.

And yet, I did not advise my cousins in Miami of my decision not to immigrate to America. Was I subconsciously playing for time? Or was this a way of letting fate take over? If only she had decided to come to America with me, how simple things would have been!

The news from the Middle East was anything but encouraging. The *Exodus,* a ship previously named the *President Warfield,* had sailed from the French port of Sete on the Mediterranean, loaded with 4,500 men and women anxious to reach Palestine. They were almost immediately detected by British destroyers on July 18, 1947. When their soldiers boarded the ship, the desperate passengers offered resistance. Three of them died and thirty were injured; the vessel itself was badly damaged.

British Foreign Secretary Bevin had the Jews transferred to another ship, the *Empire Rival,* and ordered back to Germany where they would end up in a displaced persons camp. Without intending to, Bevin had given Zionism the best possible public relations victory, clearly demonstrating the impossibility of managing the Mandate.

Because the originally proposed partition plan was stalled in the Security Council of the United Nations, the problem was thrown into the lap of the General Assembly. A United Nations Special Commission, UNSCOP was created. In the fall of 1947, they reported back to the Assembly with these suggestions:

End the Mandate

Partition Palestine into an Arab state and a Jewish state

Create an "International Zone" for Jerusalem and Bethlehem

On November 29, the Assembly by vote of 33/13 with ten abstentions accepted these proposals. Both the United States and the Soviet Union supported the resolution. A major roadblock to the eventual statehood had been overcome.

Vera wrote to me in ever more glowing terms about her new life. "We are up every morning before sunrise. We work in the fields and orange groves. It is hard work, but I am filled with pride to be a part of the birth of our nation. Our *chalutzim* come from every part of Europe. Many are survivors and nearly all have lost members of their families. Some have no one left in this world. But here, we are all one family now, supporting and helping each other, working during the day and sharing our meals at night. There are schools for the children and nurseries for the little ones. After supper, we sit around a campfire, we sing Hebrew songs and we talk late into the night of all we hope to accomplish together. I wish you were here with me."

In another letter, she mentioned the frequent clashes with Arabs in the area. "There is hardly a day when there are no casualties and weapons have been brought into the kibbutz to prepare for the coming confrontation that seems inevitable. Jacob has been named leader in charge of defending our settlement. He is really a remarkable man and everybody loves him. We are situated some ten miles east of the city of Haifa, a beautiful place on the coast and the port of arrival for the new immigrants. Have you heard from the American consul?" she added.

I had doubled my efforts to receive my teaching degree in the shortest possible time by taking additional classes and going to summer school.

In the beginning of December, we received an invitation from the American consul in Marseille to undergo a medical examination, a prerequisite to issuing that long-awaited entry visa. It was now decision time.

When I wrote to Vera, my heart was filled with sadness. I knew that I had let time and events force the decision I had been incapable or unwilling to make. I groped for words to justify that decision, to explain what truly could not be explained. How could I tell my love that our dream would never be fulfilled? I did not know why I was willing to forego the happiness of a life with Vera and I hated myself for the person I was.

The following month I received a letter form Vera. I opened it with trembling hands. "My dear, dear Leon," she wrote, "what I knew would happen, once apart from each other, did come true. Oh, how much I wish you had come with me! But I understand and I pray for you and your mother's well-being. Please pray for me too. I will never forget you and the wonderful moments we shared. With all my love, Vera."

It was on a chilly, cloudy day when we arrived at the consulate in Marseille. We passed the medical examination and were issued the visa the next day. Somehow I did not feel much like celebrating. My mother tried her best to cheer me up. "Maybe you can convince Vera to join us. It looks so hopeless over there, with the Arabs determined to deny the Jews a homeland."

I shook my head, "Vera has found her destiny. It is only in Israel that she can be truly happy."

In February I received a letter from Vera. "I hope you both are well and are preparing for that trip to America. Jacob and I got married last week. He is a good and decent man who deeply cares for me. We hope to build a life together in this land of ours, once we are allowed to live in peace. Leon, you will always have a place in my heart. May God bless you and your mother." Though this was not a completely unexpected development, the finality of that announcement filled me with overwhelming sorrow.

I decided to postpone our departure until the end of June. It was cutting it close, as the visa was to expire by July 15. However, I felt strongly that I needed the extra time to complete my studies and was determined to come to the United States with a degree that would enable me to earn a living upon arrival.

My cousins' letters were full of assurances that they would help us get started in a new environment. I visited the library, browsing through brochures about Florida. I was impressed with the natural beauty of that state, though I was also aware of the awesome power of hurricanes and the destruction they were capable of unleashing, having recently seen the results of such a storm in a newsreel.

During the remaining months of the British Mandate, which was to end on May 15, 1948, it became clear that the partition plan was doomed. David Ben-Gurion, the Jewish leader and foremost pioneer of the Zionist cause, exhorted the Jews to prepare for a full-scale attack by superior Arab forces: "The ratio between the Jews in this country and Arabs here and in the neighboring countries is 1:40. We will face seven independent Arab states: Lebanon, Syria, Trans-Jordan (an ally of the British), Iraq, and Egypt, Yemen and Saudi Arabia. They have armies; some have air forces. Egypt has a navy. This is the situation, one that confronts us with more fateful challenges than any we have faced in over eighteen hundred years."

At five o'clock in the afternoon of May 14, 1948, in the main hall of the Tel Aviv museum, a ceremony took place that inaugurated the State of Israel. It began with the singing of the Jewish anthem "Hatikvah." A few moments later, Ben-Gurion as prime minister and minister of defense of the newly created provisional government put his signature to Israel's Declaration of Independence.

The document went on to announce the establishment of the Jewish state to be known as the State of Israel. Eleven minutes after the state had been proclaimed in Tel Aviv, America's recognition was issued by Washington.

The morning of May 15, 1948 saw the British gone and Israel independent. It also was the start of a new war: the expected military intervention of five Arab states. Those attacking forces were a formidable threat as they crossed into Israel from every direction. But Israel was not unprepared. With an army of 37,000, they were ready to fight for their survival.

There were clashes everywhere. Iraqi troops had crossed the river Jordan. Syrian troops attacked from what is now known as the Golan Heights. The situation was equally grave in the Negev and critical in Jerusalem, where Trans-Jordanian soldiers were advancing from the east.

One of the fiercest battles was the one fought for the Jewish Quarter of the Old City. The Arab Legion under the command of Glubb Pasha, a British commander who had converted to Islam, succeeded in defeating the Jewish defenders of the Old City and managed to occupy the Jewish Quarter including the Wailing Wall, which represented the spiritual center of Jewish Jerusalem. These first few days were indeed days of great peril.

On May 29, Messerschitt fighter planes arrived from Czechoslovakia and the Israeli Air Force was ready to go into action. Additional Spitfires and Mosquitoes were purchased and gradually the tide turned in Israel's favor.

On June 11, a truce came into being, in response to appeals from the United Nations General Assembly. Israel was now in control of much more territory than she could have hoped for a month earlier.

By June 1, I had completed all my tests and received my teaching certificate. We now made arrangements to leave for the United States at the earliest possible time. It turned out that this meant we would have to take a ship leaving from Southampton, England on June 26.

We said good-bye to our friends in Basel and took the train across France to the port of Calais on the English Channel. After a rough crossing, we arrived in Southampton late in the evening and decided to spend the night at the hotel near the pier. The next morning, we boarded our ship, full of hope mingled with apprehension of the unknown.

The voyage was uneventful, except for one day when high waves were bouncing the ship like a toy, causing most of us to lean over the railings, green faced and in agony, praying for that torture to end.

Chapter Sixteen

America

July 4, 1948: The ocean liner S. S. *Washington* slowly, majestically, moves into New York harbor. Within minutes, the famous lady appears in all her glory, her outstretched arm holding the golden torch, bathed by the midday sun.

Straining against the ship's railing, among hundreds of passengers trying to get a first glimpse of the Statue of Liberty, that symbol of hope, we both cannot stop our tears. Tears of joy, to have finally arrived in this land of the free after the years of horror in war-torn Europe; and tears of sadness, remembering my father who died in Auschwitz and who wanted so much to come to this country. I put my arm around my mother, holding her tight.

"We made it, didn't we?" she whispered.

"Yes, my dear, we did."

The hustle bustle of that great harbor, the cacophony of ship horns and sirens from the city, and the skyscrapers that seemed to cover the entire horizon have a mesmerizing effect on the new immigrants.

In my right pants pocket is a letter I received just days before leaving Switzerland. I have read it perhaps a hundred times. Some of the ink has run on the paper, making part of the handwriting hard to read, but I know every word by heart.

It was from Jacob:

My dear Leon,

It is with unbearable sadness that I must tell you that our beloved Vera was killed in the battle of Jerusalem on May 17. My heart is broken; I cannot imagine a life without her.

We both had joined the Haganah early in May and had been assigned to a brigade charged with the defense of the Jewish Quarter in Jerusalem. Vera did

103

not have to go to the front lines. Like some of the other women, she could have taken care of the wounded, but she insisted on staying with me.

We had come under heavy artillery fire from the Jordanians and were forced to give up ground. It was a sniper's bullet that took her life, as she was just a few feet away from me. How I wish that bullet had hit me instead of that wonderful young woman, so full of life and joy.

I know how deeply you both felt for each other and I am so very sorry to have to bring you the sad news. If there is any consolation, it is the knowledge of how happy she was to participate in that great mission to build a Jewish nation. To be a pioneer for Eretz Israel.

Pray for her soul, my friend. I know we will never forget that shining star that blessed our lives for such a brief moment. May God guide you and comfort you.

Your friend, Jacob

I crumpled the letter and slowly dropped it over the railing. For a moment I watched it bobbing above the waters. Then it was gone.

Through the veil of my tears, I saw a slender gorgeous girl, her long wavy hair framing that face I knew so well, and that winsome, loving smile that captured my heart.

And I thought of all that could have been, but never was.

Epilogue

December 31, 2005, 11:45 p.m.: From the back porch of his house, an old man watches a dazzling display of brilliant fireworks lighting up the sky and ushering in the New Year.

His thoughts go back to that other night of fire crackers and Roman candles, July 4, 1948, when he and his mother, having arrived from Europe that morning, were treated to their first history lesson, the celebration of America's independence. I am that old man.

My mother has since passed on. She never remarried but found happiness doting on her grandchild and having been welcomed with open arms by her new-found family. I became part of that melting pot called the United States of America with a family of my own, a career, some hopes fulfilled, others dashed, but never forgetting that Fourth of July so long ago.

I often wondered whether any American-born person can truly imagine what it meant to start a new life in a strange land, full of opportunities, but also of pitfalls. The challenges were daunting. Not only was there a new language to master, but additional skills were often needed to successfully compete in a fast moving society.

Was I up to the task? Coming from an environment where I had been barely tolerated at best, and for the greater part of my life, persecuted and in fear for my life?

One of my first experiences in Miami, where we had settled, caused a tremendous jolt to my faith in that new-found home of mine. Waiting for a bus at the main depot on a particularly hot day, I walked over to the water fountain and started to gulp down the refreshing drink, when I was grabbed by the shoulders by a burly man who looked at me in obvious anger. "Can't you read, buster?" he called out, loudly enough to be heard by everyone in the place. He pointed to a sign above the fountain. The sign read: COLORED.

I shook my head in utter confusion. "Here," he yelled, pointing to another fountain just steps away. The sign above that fountain read: WHITE. I took a sip. The water tasted the same.

Suddenly I saw in front of me the park benches in Germany with signs written in white paint: NO JEWS ALLOWED. I remembered what led to the extermination camps and I shuddered with fear. How was it possible, I wondered, that Negroes could defend this country and die for it, but could not drink from the "white" water fountain? Or had to sit in back of the bus. Or eat at special counters in drugstores.

Over the years I have learned more about the history of these United States and the progress that needed to be made, one step at a time. I have witnessed the civil rights struggle, that excruciatingly slow path toward true emancipation and the ever-increasing concern for those who had been shortchanged all their lives. And I have come to realize that the strength of this nation lies in its unwillingness to rest on laurels. There always will be a John F. Kennedy or a Martin Luther King, Jr. saying: "We must do better!"

In the first week after our arrival and having immediately been made a part of my new family, most of whom I had never met, I started to look for work. I went to the university and applied for the position of a French teacher. The professor, a gentleman from Paris, assured me that he was not about to retire and that he did not need any assistance. My efforts to find a teaching job in the local school system and even in private schools were equally unsuccessful.

Since this was vacation time, my cousins suggested that I take a temporary job in a different field, and apply once more in the fall. I found a position with a women's clothing chain, where I started as a stockroom clerk. That temporary job would last thirty-six years.

The transition from the world of academia to the world of business proved to be less traumatic than I had feared. I was determined to make it in this country, and starting at the bottom was the path most "greenhorns" were expected to take. I became aware that there were two types of people who were successful in climbing the ladder of success. There is the "mountain climber," the future entrepreneur or CEO, the risk taker who may well fall into a crevice, but is often able to extricate himself on his way to reaching the top. But there is also what I call "the plodder," the one who climbs one hill at a time. He too will arrive, but it will take him much longer and the results may not be as spectacular. You guessed it, I belonged to that category. Eventually I moved up to assistant manager, store manager, regional supervisor and ended with a vice-presidency.

Did I regret having jettisoned my academic career? Many times. Still, Vera was perhaps right after all when she told me that I was longing for "those material rewards that life in America was all about."

Three years after coming to this country, I met a lively young woman. Renee, who like me, was born in Germany, had immigrated to America before the outbreak of the war. Since most of her schooling took place here, her English was perfect.

She is that rare combination of American spunk and European introspection. It was her upbeat view of life and her sense of humor that first attracted me to her. We have been married for fifty-five years. She is my love and my friend, and has always been guided by a deep devotion to our small family. We have a lovely daughter, Natalie, the child for whom we had been waiting for six years and who was born with a severe hearing loss. Her determination to overcome her handicap never ceases to amaze us. A brief marriage produced a son, Michael, a strapping, handsome fellow and a whiz in computers who, I am confident, will make his mark in this competitive world.

Some twenty years ago, we moved from Miami to the town of Jupiter, north of Palm Beach, where we live in a house close to the ocean. It is a quiet, laid-back type community. Lately, "progress" in the form of new developments has reached us. I hope it won't overwhelm us.

Also twenty years ago, on a sunny November morning, I finally made that trip the rabbi had admonished me to take on the day I became a bar mitzvah. It was a spur of the moment decision. A ticket became available and I found myself on the way to Israel, excited at the prospect of taking in the sights of that remarkable little country, at once young and the cradle of civilization.

I traveled along the Mediterranean, hopping from super-modern Tel-Aviv, to the beautiful port of Haifa and the sea of Tiberius. The following day it was on to Masada, where nine hundred Jews committed suicide rather than surrender to the attacking Romans.

Then, Jerusalem. There in that three-thousand-year-old city, I stood in front of the Western Wall, the holiest place in Judaism. I left a small paper with a prayer for my daughter's young son in one of the crevasses of what was once King Solomon's temple and I listened to the stones whispering to me. Back at the hotel, I browsed through some pamphlets to plan the following day's itinerary. Leafing through the brochure, I came across the description of a monument on the outskirts of Beit Shemesh, a small town twenty-five kilometers from Jerusalem. It was built in memory of 80,000 Jews deported from France and executed by the Nazis. I knew then that I had to visit that place. Early the next morning I hired a cab for the day.

After a short trip through some barren terrain, we came upon a grove nestled among towering pines. The driver pointed to a pathway. "This leads to the monument," he said. "I'll wait for you here."

Within a few steps I came upon a curved white stone wall, one hundred feet wide and twenty feet high, a stirring site in its simplicity. The words "Mémorial de la Déportation des Juifs de France" took up the entire upper part of the wall. The lower section contained the names of the 80,000 Jews who perished.

All the names were listed by "transports," indicating the date of departure of the trains from Drancy, the transit camp near Paris, and their arrival at Auschwitz two to three days later.

I was all alone in this place of sorrow and remembrance, with not another soul to share my thoughts. There was barely a breeze and no sound was heard, not even the chirping of birds.

I moved slowly along the wall, searching for the transport date that had been given to me by the Red Cross after the war: September 2, 1942. As I got closer, my hand started to shake uncontrollably. Then suddenly, I saw it: a one-line description with my father's name, Nuta Rubinstein, and his date of birth, 23.12.93 (December 23, 1893). Nothing else. A one-by-five-inch spot on that wall was my father's tombstone. For a while I just stood there, my fingers covering that space as I remembered that gentle Renaissance man who had given me so much.

As I climbed into the taxi, the driver looked at me: "Are you all right?" I nodded. We drove in silence until we reached the hotel.

When I retired from the world of business in 1984, I decided to go back to my first calling: teaching.

After my discovery of the Raoul Wallenberg Park across from the United Nations with its plaque remembering the six million, I embarked on a thorough study of the history of the Holocaust by reading the works of leading historians who covered that period; Raul Hilberg, David Wyman, Elie Wiesel, Nora Levin, and my friend, the former project director of the United States Holocaust Memorial Museum, Michael Berenbaum, were among the ones whose words and thoughts prompted me to contact the local school system, which recently had incorporated the teaching of the Holocaust into their curriculum.

It was a story that needed telling and I wanted to be among those who told it. I have since spoken to thousands of young people between the ages of ten and eighteen. Upon entering the classroom, I walk straight up to the blackboard and write down a formula:

PREJUDICE + DISCRIMINATION +
PERSECUTION = EXTERMINATION

And I tell my young audience of those days of darkness and despair, when unspeakable evil engulfed the world.

Before sharing with them my incredible escape into Switzerland, I challenge them to tell me about their own prejudices. When I ask them to raise their hands if they have never used the "N word" or called a classmate a "retard," no hands went up. This does not surprise me.

"I'd like to tell you a story," I continue, "of a man sitting in a wheelchair in Cambridge, England, unable to move, unable to speak, who must project some inaudible sounds through a contraption that converts them into words on a computer screen. If you see this man, you will probably make a wide circle around him, for he is obviously a cripple, perhaps retarded. Does anyone know who this is?"

A hand goes up. "Stephen Hawking," a youngster will announce proudly. Indeed, only the greatest living astrophysicist since Albert Einstein. Prejudice, I explain, means to pre-judge. To form an opinion based on hearsay, misjudgments, and outright lies.

Sometimes I am invited to speak to the "gifted classes." They are indeed among the brightest and most mature of the students. When I tell them that this label alone does not impress me, they look surprised. I pull out a letter Chaim Ginott, the well-known educator, wrote to his fellow teachers in 1972:

Dear Teacher:
  I am a survivor of the concentration camp. My eyes saw what no man should witness.
  Gas chambers built by Learned engineers.
  Children poisoned by Educated physicians.
  Infants killed by Trained nurses.
  Women and babies shot and burned by high school and college graduates.
  So I am suspicious of education.
  My request is: Help your students become human. Your efforts must never produce learned monsters, skilled psychopaths, educated Eichmanns. Reading, writing, and arithmetic are important only, if they serve to make our children more human.

I tell them of the Wannsee Conference near Berlin on January 20, 1942 where fifteen Nazi leaders, half of them with doctorates decided in just ninety minutes to exterminate the Jews of Europe. I remind them that the truly gifted is the one who uses his abilities and skills to help his fellow men and who will be a leader in that quest for a better tomorrow.

Then I talk about a trip I took to Auschwitz a few years back. Though the wire surrounding the compound was no longer electrified, my heart was suddenly filled with fear as I entered the gate with its sign "Arbeit Macht Frei," that cruel hoax of depraved minds. I walked through the gas chamber and I saw the ovens.

I stood where my father must have stood when they selected him for extermination. I remember the glass showcase filled with thousands of shoes
taken from the victims. And I can't get out of my mind that pink booty on top
of the heap. One-and-a-half million children perished in the Holocaust. "It is
a number impossible to comprehend," I tell them. "I shall try to make it easier for you to understand. Most of the killings took place during 1942–43 and
44. This means 500,000 each year or 1,500 a day.

Does that number mean anything to you?"

A hand goes up. "The number of students in our school," a boy says in a
barely audible voice.

I nod. "Every day of every week of every month of every year for three
years, an ENTIRE SCHOOL DISAPPEARED. Imagine your school empty of
all life, with nothing left but silence." That they can understand. And they
walk up to the board and shake my hand and I hug them.

Soon after my visit, letters and poems arrive from my young friends. Their
expression of empathy, their sincerity in wanting to help make this a better
world, deeply touches me. I have selected just one letter, though all of them
show a maturity that belies their ages:

Dear Mr. Rubinstein,
    My grandfather was one of the U.S. soldiers in the war that cost so many their
lives. I have heard his stories and I have read books like Anne Frank since the
fourth grade. Although I try to feel what you must have felt, I cannot even come
close. I have lost a loved one, but she was not taken with such brutality. My an-
cestors were Poles and that makes me feel even worse knowing that your father
and millions of others died in my homeland.
    I cannot match your pain, but I can try to understand. I feel when people like
you come to our school and teach people like me, they are doing a huge favor
to the world. This story should not and I hope will not be forgotten. I leave you
with this promise I shall tell my kids and grand kids about you and about all who
were hurt or killed in this terrible war.
Sincerely,
Christine L. Petersen
Sixth grade student at St. Clare School, Lake Park, Florida

I leave the children with an anecdote: A famous rabbi once was asked by
one of his brightest students: "Rabbi, if you were to give us just a few words
of wisdom to live by, what would they be?"

And the rabbi replied: "Be honest, so you can live with yourself. Be com-
passionate, so others can live with you."

"But where is God in all of this?" the student wanted to know.

The rabbi smiled: "He will be very pleased if you follow my advice."

Talking to these youngsters is getting a little harder every year now. Yet it fills me with such contentment. When I look into their eyes, those serious eyes, I see innocence and I see wisdom—and a determination to fight prejudice early on.

Perhaps I have struck a chord.

How then can I possibly quit?

I can't. Not yet.

About the Author

Leon Rubinstein, born in Frankfurt, fled Germany with his parents in 1933 after the rise of the Nazis and lived in Luxembourg, Brussels, and southern France. In 1942, after his father's arrest and deportation, he and his mother escaped across the Alps to Switzerland. In Switzerland, he studied at the Faculty of Philosophy and History at the University of Basel and earned his teaching degree. After the war, he immigrated to the United States where he switched to the business world and had a successful career with a national chain of retail stores. For the past twenty years, he has written op-ed pieces for Florida newspapers and spoken to students throughout the Florida school system about the Holocaust and his own remarkable story of flight and escape. He and his wife live in Jupiter, Florida.